ON TRACK

Henry Gittins – Railway Pioneer in Siam & Canada

Henry Gittins as Director of the Southern Route during 1909-1917.
(From The 60th anniversary of Royal Thai Railways souvenir book, 1957. Private collection).

ON TRACK

HENRY GITTINS – RAILWAY PIONEER IN SIAM & CANADA

Paul Gittins

RIVER
BOOKS

First published and distributed in 2014 by
River Books
396 Maharaj Road, Tatien, Bangkok 10200
Tel. 66 2 622-1900, 224-6686
Fax. 66 2 225-3861
E-mail: order@riverbooksbk.com
www.riverbooksbk.com

Editor: Narisa Chakrabongse
Production supervision: Paisarn Piemmettawat
Design: Ruetairat Nanta

ISBN 978 616 7339 42 9

Printed and bound in Thailand by Bangkok Printing Co., Ltd.

CONTENTS

Acknowledgements   7

Foreword   8

Prelude   10

Surveying and sickness   12

Canada   28

Colleagues and customs   50

Royal Line Opening and Home Leave   60

Mayhem and Marriage   70

Law and Order   78

The Discovery of Hua Hin   92

Promotion and Protocol   108

The Southern Line and World War I   114

Retirement   130

Postscript   138

Appendix   140

Glossary of Colloquial & Slang Terms of The Time   146

Bibliography   147

Index   148

To bring the dead to life

Is no great magic.

Few are wholly dead:

Blow on a dead man's embers

And a live flame will start.

From *"To Bring the Dead to Life"*
by Robert Graves

ACKNOWLEDGEMENTS

I would like to thank my brother Michael for his many suggestions and help with the text, my brother David for providing much archive material, my aunt Rashne Gittins for her comments about my grandfather's retirement in Devon and my nephew Yan Gittins for help with the photographs.

I owe thanks also to Rainer Fehrmann and his brother Bengel for information concerning the hiding of weapons during the internment episode in July 1917.

My cousin, Jan Heslop, provided the memory of Henry Gittins in his retirement always ready to help anyone in need.

I would also like to thank Andrew Pinder for his illustrations and help with arranging the text, Susan Drake for her helpful suggestions and Tew Bunnag for his encouragement and advice.

FOREWORD

First hand accounts of how railway lines were built are invariably interesting. There are all too few. We hear frequently of stories of the life and times of the chief engineers and the locomotive builders, but rarely about the men who built the lines that first criss-crossed the world in the 19th. century. Henry Gittins experienced all parts of the process across two continents, from labouring in Canada to running a huge construction process in Siam, and his memoirs are therefore invaluable in adding to our knowledge.

This is part of a wider history that is all too often forgotten. The growth of the railways across the world was a quite remarkable and rapid development. Between the opening of the first railway in England, the Liverpool & Manchester in 1830, and the outbreak of the First World war, more than a million kilometres of line were built, with tracks appearing in almost every country of the world. The railways were the greatest industry during much of this period, leading to the creation of huge corporations that for a time were the largest in the world and undoubtedly had the widest effect of any technological change.

As Paul Gittins says in the book, 'The modern world was replacing the old and one of the major factors accelerating this change was the expansion of the railways on which my grandfather was later to work.' While Henry Gittins was involved in the tail end of the development of railways, it is nevertheless quite extraordinary that people just two generations back were taking part in that process.

It is almost impossible to exaggerate the impact of the arrival of the railways. The book cites an example of local products from Nong Khai province, such as hand-woven cloth, gum collected from trees and animal skins, being sent down to Khorat by bullock cart. The journey might take between sixteen and thirty days, and possibly much longer in the wet season. Yet by rail it would take a day or so. Multiply that change across a nation, indeed across the whole world, and one begins to get the idea of how railways transformed almost everything about the way people lived, all in a very short period of time. When the railway arrived, for the first time people could travel faster than a horse could be ridden and that enabled them to cover far longer distances than ever before. The railways broke the isolation of a myriad of communities and, again, in an apposite example quoted in the book, the corrupt local authorities in the Siamese hinterland became more accountable. It is no coincidence that democracy grew hand in hand across the world along with the railways.

There was a price to pay, however, and some of the story is shocking. There are numerous deaths which are written about almost casually because they are so commonplace. On the main line built from Bangkok to Khorat over the space of eight and a half years, thirty-five Europeans and seven thousand coolies died, although Henry Gittins reckoned it was more like ten thousand. The difficulties faced by the builders cannot be overestimated and running a railway in the tropics, where monsoon rains can wash away a line in a matter of hours, was no easy task either. The very matter of fact way in which Henry Gittins describes all these events actually strengthens the impact of the account. This is the real story of an Englishman abroad, sanguine and calm in the face of great challenges.

It is indeed a compelling tale.

Christian Wolmar
Author of 'Blood, Iron and Gold.
How the railways transformed the world.'

PRELUDE

The summer of 2009 in Majorca broke late, but made up for its lateness with several days of torrential rain. It was during one of those days that I remembered my grandfather's diaries of his years in Siam, still lying in the drawer in which I had put them many years ago. Not that I had entirely forgotten them as I had tried reading them now and again but been defeated by his flowing italic handwriting which made all the letters look the same. This time, though, I would really try and do better. I took one of the diaries and opening it at random, began hesitantly to read.

September 12th. 1905. A coolie down with dysentery, a common thing and would not be noticed here but for the extraordinary treatment he received from the priests. He had been doctored by us and was slowly pulling around and probably would have completely recovered had it not been that he listened to the advice of his friends and called in the priest. He came late in the evening and decided that the sickness was caused by a devil and 'twas absolutely necessary that the devil be driven out and set to work to do it.

He started by giving him a dose of chillies and water with some holy candle wax inside it. This brought up something but not the devil. He then doused him from head to foot with buckets of cold water until the man shrivelled up and became limp and speechless. Still the devil did not show up. He then obtained a stick with a nail in the end and jabbed him all over the body and legs, drawing blood at each poke, meanwhile praying and exhorting as hard as he could. 'What devil are you? Where do you come from? Why do you trouble this man?' etc. This treatment effectually expelled the devil and the man's life at the same time, and not to be wondered at.

Fee paid to the priest and collected from the coolies amounted to 9 tics.

I paused in my reading, wondering if the incident had been somewhat embroidered. But my grandfather was, as I was to find out more fully, a very down-to-earth person and not one to exaggerate. I also had another source of information, the Times obituary of February 13th. 1937, which after detailing his 'remarkable career as organizer and builder of railways in Siam' ended by describing him as 'slight, erect, alert of eye and movement ..... He read much and had leanings towards poetry and romance, which he concealed from the public behind a certain brusqueness of manner and deportment.....'

Every bit of information now spurred me on to find out more about my grandfather, my only regret being that I had never known him. Well, I would do the next best thing – get to know him through his diaries and the memoir that he wrote later in life about his early adventures in Canada.

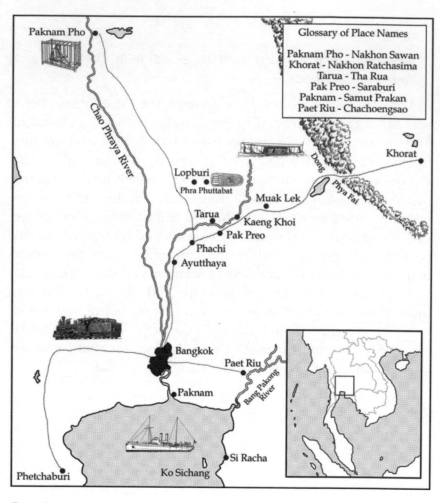

First railway routes.

CHAPTER ONE
Surveying & Sickness

The second half of the nineteenth century, with its expanding colonial powers, provided many openings for doctors, teachers, engineers, forestry officials, missionaries and administrators to take up employment in distant lands. Amongst these countries offering opportunities was Siam, although it was only just emerging from feudalism and opening itself up to western influences under its reforming monarchs, King Mongkut, who reigned from 1851-1868 and his successor King Chulalongkorn from 1868-1910.

In his efforts to modernize Siam, King Mongkut had cultivated the European powers through treaties and diplomacy and brought in European governesses to educate his children. But he was careful not to let any one colonial power get too strong a foothold in his country and when, in 1855, Queen Victoria sent him a model train (now in the Bangkok National Museum) and tried to persuade him to let the British East India company finance a railroad in Siam, he declined the proposal. But plans for a railway system that was so essential to the modernization of Siam were only put on hold. In 1888, King Chulalongkorn commissioned a British firm of civil engineers, Messrs. Punchard, Mactaggart & Lowther to carry out a survey for a railroad from Bangkok to Ayutthaya and on to Khorat, which would be the first phase in a national system. Khorat, located at the western edge of the Khorat plateau was approximately two hundred and sixty kilometres from Bangkok and was an important gateway to the provinces in the north-east.

My grandfather (who had previously worked in Canada for four years, the last two with the Canadian Pacific Railways) was one of the Punchard survey team under the charge of

William Galway, the Chief Engineer. He was engaged for three years as assistant engineer with a monthly salary of £26. (This sum had risen to £40 per month by August 1890).

The contract for his employment stipulated that, as part of the agreement, 10% of his salary was to be retained in an escrow account as security against any breach of contract until the amount deposited had attained £60. This was to cover any fines that might be incurred by the employee for any 'breach of regulations or any intemperance, insubordination, malingering or other misconduct.....' In grandfather's case this was rather a superfluous requirement as he was always a model employee as William Galway acknowledged in his final letter after the completion of the Punchard survey when he wished him 'the success in your profession which your energy and ability justly entitle you to.'

The first party of Railway Surveyors in Siam, 1888.
(Sitting: Henry Gittins, 2nd. from left. Standing: Smiles, end left.)

Unfortunately, my grandfather's diaries covering the survey period were lost. But in his book, 'Surveying and Exploring in Siam', James McCarthy, who was involved in the demarcation of the northern frontiers of Siam, noted that the 'whole of these railway surveys were completed without an accident' despite the difficulties of communication and travel and the general lawlessness of the times – factors which grandfather was to encounter and describe in his existing diaries which began in 1892, when following the end of the Punchard survey, he started work with a British constructor, George Murray Campbell, who had been awarded the contract to build the line from Bangkok to Khorat.

My grandfather was then thirty-three years old and through the experience gained in the Punchard survey was now very much his own man, confident in his abilities and prepared to be critical of others both on a personal and professional level. Much of this critical attitude can be attributed to the rivalry between British and German personnel in the Railway Department as a result of the foreign policy of King Chulalongkorn who, sandwiched between the French in Indo-China and the British who controlled Burma on his northern and western sides, was intent in playing one off against the other. To this end, he offered a stake in the economic development of Siam to both Britain and Germany through the development of a railway system in the hope that this would give them sufficient vested interest to keep France at bay, while at the same time offsetting Britain and Germany against each other to prevent either of them becoming too dominant.

In terms of diplomacy, this strategy was successful in keeping Siam as an independent kingdom, in spite of some later territorial concessions to both the French and the British. In practice, however, it led to much bickering between the British and German contingents over the awarding of contracts and the day-to-day running of affairs, especially as in 1890 a Railways Department had been established under the Directorship of a German, Karl Bethge. The latter (an elderly but experienced engineer who had previously represented the German government in China) was far from happy with the Bangkok-Khorat contract going to a British contractor and it was in this atmosphere of tension and rivalry that the diaries begin in 1892.

In the early part of that year, it appears that my grandfather, although working for George Murray Campbell on the early construction of the Bangkok-Khorat line had applied for a post in the newly established Royal Railways Department – probably because the pay was better. His first attempt was spectacularly unsuccessful. In a later note to his diaries, he recalled this episode.

> I had sent him (Bethge) a letter asking for a post in the new Department and this was under consideration when I happened to meet him in Matthewson's house. The latter had been one of Punchard's men and was then in the Public Works. Bethge came in with the remark that 'I am very tired. I have been correcting Punchard's plans.'
>
> This got my back up and I said, 'What do you know of Punchard's plans. You have never been over the line and know nothing of the country' and a bit more. This naturally got his back up and he bounced out with some remarks. Naturally, I suppose, I received a reply next day that my services were not required.

A little later, another clash with a German colleague resulted perversely in achieving his objective. He was up in the Khorat hills, where he was in charge of the Pak Preo-Kaeng Khoi Section, when he was visited by the Chief Engineer called Rohns, who wanted to be shown work on the line, to which grandfather replied that he would only show him the part for which he was responsible and no more.

He got very excited, saying he was the Chief Engineer and would not be talked to like that. I must obey his instructions. We talked and eventually he said, 'Would you like to join the department?' I replied, 'Certainly, if you can arrange with Campbell and give me a better salary.' Five hundred tics[1] per month, if I remember rightly and one hundred tics field allowance. To this he agreed.

I can only assume that after Rohns had calmed down, he began to appreciate the good work that grandfather was doing, which led him to make the offer of the transfer. It was not the only thing that grandfather recorded about the visit.

I remember that trip, for in their usual fashion the bearers all struggled into camp as they pleased, some soon, some late. This annoyed Rohns for his beer came in about the last and there was a lot of "donnerwettering" to his assistant, a man called Altman, and instructions: 'Tomorrow morning, Herr Altman, you will start the men off, separating each by two minutes, and you will see that this order is kept.'

I told him that this was no use for the men would go their own customary way. To which he replied, 'In Germany, we would shoot them if they did not obey orders.' Eventually, he agreed to our way of leaving the men alone and all went well. But Rohns' hankering after all things German showed itself again when they came to a rather high and open spot in the jungle and his first remark was, *'Mr. Gittins, if this was Germany, there would be a beer garden sited here.'*

Henry Gittins on line c. 1890.

17

If, at times, my grandfather found it difficult to get on with his German colleagues, it was as nothing compared to the difficulties he faced in dealing with the Siamese climate and the conditions of his work. Just getting from one place to another was a lengthy and uncomfortable process. Travel was either by boat up or down river or on foot along jungle trails. His diary entries for June 1892, when he took up his first posting under the R.R.D. as Section Engineer of the hill division in the Hinlap area near Pak Preo, make grim reading.

12th. *Left Bangkok on the 9th. by Chao Phraya[2] river for Ayutthaya. Reached there at 4.0 and stayed overnight at MacGlashan's. At Ayutthaya all day. Left in the morning of the 11th. for Pak Preo. Towed to Tarua by steam launch. Reached Pak Preo on the 12th. at 7.0 and stayed the day arranging for boats to Kaeng Khoi. Heavy rain at night.*

13th. *Left at 7.0 for Kaeng Khoi. Sent outfit on by boat. Took pony along, but found the trail too wet to ride him – wet and sloppy the whole way. Reached Kaeng Khoi at 10.0 p.m.*

15th. *Left at 7.15 for Hinlap. Arrived at 12.15. Men returned for remainder of outfit. Rain at night.*

16th. *Remainder of outfit arrived. Rain at night.*

17th. *On line. Traversing[3] old location, commencing at km.10.*

19th. *Sunday. In camp all day, plotting up traverse.*

20th. *Traversing. 2-3 kms. Long day, missed the track coming back and nearly got lost...Rain at night.*

22nd. *On line traversing. Felt a little off colour in the evening. Heavy rain at night. Two men down with fever for the past two or three days.*

23rd.. *In doors all day, plotting, etc. Felt somewhat dicky, so stayed in. Men cutting stakes. Rain in afternoon.*

25th. *Staking out permanent location. Finished at 9.20 kms.*

29th. *Cook and two boys down with fever.*

30th. *Down with fever or something. Went down line. Lambert* (his colleague) *levelling.[4] Returned at 12.0 Heavy Rain.*

July 1st. *On line. Self not very bright. Cook and several men down with fever.*

4th. *Self and Lambert both seedy, so decided to pull out.*

But having made the decision to 'pull out', they were still several days from Bangkok and proper medical attention.

6th. *Left at 7.30 for Kaeng Khoi. Self riding on a stretcher carried by four men. Reached Kaeng Khoi about 5.0, tired out and damned bad.*

7th.. *Paid off men and left at 12.0. Reached Pak Preo at 4.0. Met Mr.& Mrs.Knight of Campbells. Stayed the night. Self bad and wandering.*

8th. *Left at 5.30. No breakfast. Missed launch at Tarua. Cook's boat as usual way behind. Rowed on towards Ayutthaya. Stopped for food at native village on the way. Started again and got drenched about half an hour afterwards. So made for a big Chinese boat. They gave us food and shelter and some dry blankets. Both we and our dunnage soaked and both of us about as bad as we could be.*

9th. *Left at 5.0. and got to Ayuthaya at 12.0. Stayed with Campbell's doctor overnight. I was about as bad all day as I want to be and wandered again.*

10th..   *Left by Chao Phraya, feeling very bad. Reached Bangkok at 2.30 and went or was taken by the skipper to the hospital.*

11th..   *Dr. Gowan injected quinine into my leg. Fever much better.*

But from now on, he could echo James McCarthy's complaint that 'fever had now established itself in my system and became my annual companion.' He stayed at the hospital until the 16th, his convalescence not being helped by the doctor having touched a nerve in his leg with the injection, which half paralysed the leg for three days. By the 24th. however, he was back at the R.R.D. office and sufficiently recovered to have an argument with Rohns over a technical matter, with the latter eventually backing down. At the beginning of August, he managed to get leave to go to Ko Sichang for a month to complete his convalescence. Ko Sichang, an island about seven hours south of Bangkok by steamship, was in the process of being developed as a resort by the royal family and princes. With his surveyor's skills, he was not impressed.

They are making roads, parks and erecting shanties all over the place and in such a gimcrack way that the whole of it will have to be done over again in a couple of years. The roads are already sinking and big holes looming up. The main road changes its name about every one hundred yards. Every creek, bridge, path, etc. possesses a name, painted with white letters on a blue background on tin and tacked to a board. The King's bodyguard are down here under canvas, that is to say a piece of brown canvas thrown over a ridge pole and no more fit to shelter men from heavy rain than brown paper. From the palace down along the main road past the Hotel, the stinks are many, sewage and others. There's no water on the island, and altho' they have been boring for some time, they have only succeeded in breaking their boring tools. The water is brought from Bangkok. The natives use rain water. What they do in the dry season I don't know. The place is pretty enough but fit for nothing being nearly all rock. Why the Siamese are wasting money in erecting palaces, building roads, piers and God knows what, no one knows. But for money wasting it's hard to beat.

The month's convalescence ended, grandfather went back on the line, but was soon under the weather again. An entry at the beginning of September when he was returning to camp for the night shows the state he was in.

Got played out before I arrived and only just managed to crawl. Have not got over the fever yet and my legs seem to belong to a child. He was not much better a few days later. *Getting on slowly but shaky about the hands and can't write. Am leaving.*

Back at the office in Bangkok, he was still feeling very shaky.

Was more or less off colour all the month of September. Dr.Gowan gave me tincture of nux vomica to pull my nerves together. Even celebrations for the King's birthday could not raise his spirits. *The King's birthday was celebrated on the Twenty-first. River and streets illuminated, but it made no difference to me – decorations spoilt by the rain, which was almost incessant for three days.*

At the end of October, he returned to Hinlap, taking a week to arrive, travelling up river by launch and chow.[5] But the malarial district of Hinlap soon started to take its toll on his health again.

On line every day ..... a little off colour occasionally but not enough to prevent working .....had several touches of fever. Generally had a slight attack for five or six hours in the afternoon and evening every three or four days. But

Chow River boat.

still he pressed on. The entry for the 19th. December 1892 states that he was *on line all day, locating and traversing. Finished to Km. 142.7*

Christmas Day brought no respite as he was still feeling below par and his mood not helped by the arrival of a German colleague.

> *Kaeppler, a fat German engineer arrived at 5.0 pm. Don't think much of him. A useless devil. His main object seems to be drinking beer.*

By now, grandfather's English colleague, Lambert, was too sick to continue and left for Bangkok. A few days later, grandfather *'very dicky and off his feed'* followed and on the 4th. January 1893 reached Bangkok and went straight to hospital where he was told by Dr. Hayes that he should not return to the hills as he was chock full of malaria and had an enlarged spleen, which was always liable (if he got fever) to return.

After a week in hospital and a few days convalescence, he returned to the office, where Rohns asked him to take over the Bangkok Section as things were in great trouble. Although a compliment to grandfather, this new assignment meant closer contact with Rohns, with whom he had had several differences of opinion before. Matters soon came to a head.

> *At the end of January, I resigned my appointment on the Railway staff, or should I say, I gave three months notice. Had a row with Rohns over many things, so thought it better to chuck it.* This might have been the end of grandfather's career in the railways. *But instead in April, when my time expired, he (Rohns) asked me to stay on and as Bethge had returned whom I found a more sensible man to pull with and they agreed to my conditions, I thought I could not do better.*

So for the first few months of 1893, he stayed in Bangkok, apart from a few weeks spent back at Hinlap finishing up Kaeppler's work. In July, he was granted three months leave of absence to pick up his health in Hong Kong. But just before he left, he witnessed the outbreak of hostilities between the French and the Siamese in the so-called Paknam Incident.

The French, looking to expand their influence in Indo-China, demanded that the Siamese give up their claims to suzerainty over Laos and sent the gunboat 'Lutin' to Bangkok to reinforce their demands. Initially, the Siamese were not prepared to make any concessions, which led to some skirmishing in the disputed area.

> *Great excitement in Bangkok the early part of July over the French Question. The French threatened to send gunboats up to Bangkok. Of course, the Siamese laughed at it and considered the forts at Paknam* (modern day Samut Prakan) *could not be passed by all the gunboats in creation. Great talk of war, buying arms and ammunition, massing troops, laying mines and sinking junks and lighters at the mouth of the river to block the channel.*

But the French were not bluffing and sent two more boats up the Chao Phraya without the permission of the Siamese, which was a statutory requirement for all boats proceeding up to Bangkok. Grandfather goes on to describe what happened next.

In spite of forts, preparations and the rest of it, on the night of the 13th. July, two gunboats, the 'Inconstant' and the 'Comete' passed the forts and three Siamese gunboats, badly peppering the forts and two of the gunboats, killing several Siamese and wounding fifteen or twenty. On the French side, three killed and two or three wounded.

Having forced their way up river, the French gunboats trained their guns on the Royal Palace, at the same time delivering an ultimatum that the Siamese must give up Laos. It was at this point in the confrontation that grandfather left for Hong Kong, or rather attempted to leave because the French now stepped up the pressure on the government by blockading the Siamese coast.

25th. *Left Bangkok on the 'Loo Sook' for Hong Kong ..... A lot of lighters and junks sunk across the mouth of the river, leaving a passage in the centre about two hundred yards wide ..... dropped anchor at Ko Sichang at 6.45.*

26th. *At Ko Sichang. French gunboat arrived in morning. Sent two boatloads of men ashore and hoisted the French flag on the Royal flag staff.*

27th. *The French hoisted their flag on the Customs House, also on the small island opposite and on the flag staff on the peak. From the point, they also flew the blockade signal. An ensign came aboard and informed us that the port of Bangkok would be blockaded after midnight on the 28th*

Another French johnnie, a Lieutenant with finger nails half an inch long, came aboard and

Hong Kong 1893.

> *said the blockade would not commence until 5.0*
> *pm of the 29th., by which time we had to clear out.*

Not wanting to delay any further, they left the same day for Hong Kong.

August 3rd *Arrived at Hong Kong and put up at the Hong Kong Hotel, a fine building of five stories. Elevator, hot and cold baths and everything complete for $5 a day.*

4th. *Having felt somewhat out of sorts for some time past, thought I could not do better than consult Dr. Cantlie, who seems the best man here. Told me my spleen was an enormous size and that I was generally full up with malaria. Advised me to go up to a small hospital he has at the Peak and with a few weeks rest and careful treatment would probably make a complete cure of me.*

5th. *Removed to the Peak.*

6th. *Bad during the night, ague and fever, temp. up to 105 degrees. Took a draught of something, camphor with pyrene and another drug.*

7th.   Had a hot bath and the Jap attendant rubbed in some ointment and massaged the spleen, night and morning. Took 50 grains quinine.

8th.   Better today. More hot baths, more massage. Took 40 grains quinine and an arsenic pill after meals.

9th.   Still improving. Hot baths and massage as yesterday. 30 grains quinine and 3 arsenic pills. Went down town by chair and tram.

10th. As yesterday. Took 15 grains quinine and 2 arsenic pills. 135 grains of quinine in 4 days ain't bad.

11th. Improving rapidly. Spleen nearly all gone. Dr. Cantlie painted up my chest like a Red Indian and then took a copy of it on muslin. This spleen seems to have been a rather interesting case to him. More than 'twas to me. Weather very fine upon the hill and much cooler than in the town. Took 10 grains of quinine. 2 pills.

By Sunday the 13th., he was down to one pill and increasing his walking exercise.

> Walked down to Aberdeen, a village at the foot of the hill on the south-east side 1330 feet below. A long climb up, winding path and fairly good walking. One hour going down and one hour ten minutes pulling up. Felt somewhat played out on reaching the summit........

He notes rather disapprovingly that *the people go about in solid comfort here, carried in chairs by two or four coolies. Seems to be very little walking done.*

With time on his hands, it would have been surprising if my grandfather had not spent some moments in taking stock of his life and perhaps thinking back to the events in his life

Peak Hospital (centre of photo).

that had brought him to Siam, starting with when he first left England as a young man in 1881 to travel to Canada in search of adventure and which he recalled in the memoirs that he wrote later on in his life when he was retired.

Notes

1. A 'tic' was the European abbreviation for a tical, the Siamese unit of currency. In the 1880s, 10 ticals equalled £1 but had risen to 13 by the turn of the century.

   'Field allowance' was made to those working in a camping situation with no access to facilities or services.

2. Chao Phraya – the greatest river of Siam, formerly known as the Menam. It begins at Nakhon Sawan (where the Ping and Nan rivers join) and flows south for two hundred and thirty miles through the low alluvial plain in the centre of the country and then on to the Gulf of Thailand.

3. Traversing – 'a line of survey plotted from compass bearings and measured distances between successive points.' O.E.D.

4. Levelling – 'ascertaining the differences of level in a piece of land.' O.E.D.

5. Chow – a boat on which the rower stands facing the bow with the oar swivelling on a small upright, fixed on the edge of the boat.

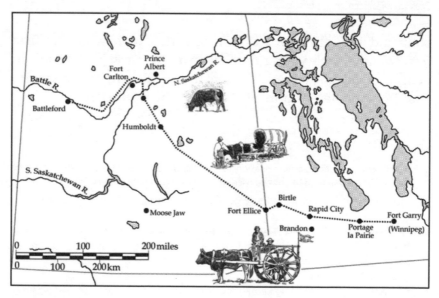

Map Canada.

CHAPTER TWO
CANADA

The 1880s in Canada saw an increasing influx of immigrant workers, fortune seekers and adventurers following the expansion of the railways into the interior of Canada, known as the Prairie West, a vast area bounded roughly by Lake Superior and the Rocky mountains. Amongst them was my grandfather, aged twenty-three, who sailed from Liverpool on the S.S. Polynesian for Quebec on the 14th. July 1881. The day before, he had left his family home in Clifton, where his father was the manager of the Clifton Downs Hotel and travelled up from Bristol to Liverpool on the 'old Parliamentary penny-a-miler', taking a third class fare for 13s.8d.

The seats had no cushions and the backs were a bit hard. No heating beyond what you got from a foot warmer, a flat tin full of hot water for which you paid a shilling, the lighting consisting of an oil lamp dropped through the roof with a glass bowl, which bowl collected the droppings of the oil and swished it about from side to side as the train travelled .....Those were the days of no lavatories on the trains and single compartments 1st, 2nd and 3rd or parliamentary class, in which you were locked in, for the guard often locked the door before starting. So common was this that many , especially commercial travellers, carried a key to avoid waiting for the door to be unlocked on arrival.

His last night had been spent sharing a room with his father in the Adelphi Hotel at Liverpool. He left no record of any farewell conversations but did note that they both caught a flea the next morning when dressing. Little did he know at that stage that this would be as nothing compared with some of the lodgings that he was to encounter in the times ahead of him. Ever the careful man with his money, he recorded that his capital when leaving England was £20 in a draft and £5.12.0 in cash, which had to keep him until he found a job. The cost of the fare was £12 and the voyage took ten days.

On arrival in Quebec, my grandfather, who had trained as an architect, tried to find work in an architect's practice but with no success. Montreal was no better and so he decided to try his luck in Toronto.

> The streets of Toronto in those days were mostly paved with round cedar wood blocks, not square, the trunks and branches when big enough being just sawn across. This meant logs of all sizes laid on the ground with not much of a formation and the crevices filled in with sand and gravel. The side walks were of planks – all well enough when newly laid but not after a little wear when holes appeared and you jammed your toes against projecting nails or damaged your leg through a misplaced or rotten plank.

It seems that his efforts to find work paid off and he found a job in an architect's office (Darling & Curry) at a salary of $40 a month, helping prepare plans for a competition for the new Parliament buildings in Toronto. Toronto was also to give my grandfather the first indication of how cold winter in Canada could be, as although the office was heated with steam radiators, his lodgings were not, so that the water froze solid in his jug.

> The early part of January was bitterly cold. The temperature went down to 20 degrees below on the 24th. January. Went to the office with my ears wrapped up in a silk handkerchief, they being very swollen from the effects of the previous day's frostbite.

Unfortunately, the practice did not win the competition for the new Parliament buildings with the result that work in the office tailed off. But an offer of a job in another architect's practice in Portage la Prairie, some forty-five miles west of Winnipeg, found my grandfather on the move again and in February 1882, he started work for Soule & Dalamain at double the salary he'd had in Toronto. He seems to have got on well with Dalamain and when in May of that year the practice was dissolved, the two of them made the momentous decision of 'going west', a decision which my grandfather describes in characteristically matter-of-fact terms.

With nothing else in view, we decided to go West, following up the old advice "Go West, young man and grow up with the country".

They were, of course, following the pioneer's great dream – that of going west to start a new life - a dream encouraged by the Canadian Government in the Dominion Lands Act of 1872 which encouraged settlers to take on homesteads comprising 160 acres for the payment of a small fee of $10, with the stipulation that they had to construct a residence and cultivate a certain area annually. Not that either of them, I think, were considering becoming settlers. It was more the idea and challenge of the journey that must have caught their imagination.

The next thing was to decide on the outfit and start purchasing it, resulting in one ox $90, harness and hobbles $10.25, cart and cover $22, tent 8 x 10 $16.50, groceries $25.25, hardware $17.40. A total of $181.40. In addition we each had a buffalo robe $12 and a pair of blankets $5. Dalamain being a vegetarian we had no tinned meat beyond two or three bought for emergencies... and an occasional duck or other game bird shot on the way... Our principal food was haricot beans and dried *peas, boiled to a soup, Graham flour (the ordinary brown) and dried apple rings and very toothsome food too. Tea, of course, was the liquid. For bread we made a kind of damper in a frying pan. A bit stodgy I rather think.*

As for the route they were going to take, the Canadian Pacific Railways in those days had just passed a little to the west of Brandon and was pushing across the Prairie to the Rockies.

There was little or no settlement ahead, but there was to the North with several rising villages, Rapid City, Birtle, Fort Ellice, etc... and further on Humboldt and Clarkes Crossing, a ferry over the South branch of the Saskatchewan River, and this decided us on the route and also because 'twas the old trail.[1] To Fort Ellice a fair lot of land had been taken up and cultivation started. Beyond that point hardly any, until you got to Battleford.

Before they left, Dalamain and my grandfather had met up with an English family from Gloucestershire, Mr. and Mrs. Soulter and their son and daughter who had a homestead at Portage la Prairie. They must have become quite friendly with them as the family gave them a parting cheer when they pulled out with the ox and cart and attached a small flag worked by Miss Soulter with the lines "To the Rockies or Bust". Mr Soulter waved them off with some verses that he had written, which grandfather kept and at a later date must have pasted into his diary.

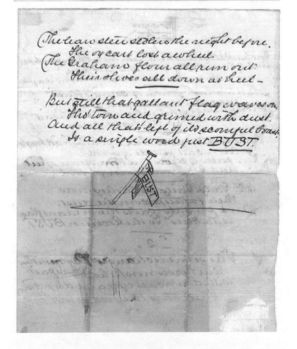

TO THE ROCKIES
BUST.

1

Now hark all ye who list to hear our noble England's praise,
And of the noble things her sons have done,
In these mad modern days,
When two rash youths of boyhood flush,
And full of courage rare,
From Portage start with gladsome heart
And never a thought or care.

A half starved ox these youths had bought,
An ox cart made of wood,
Two pairs of olives – just one clean shirt
And Graham flour for food.

Oh! Daily Daily walk they now,
Their footsteps scorn the dust:
And proudly waves the verdant flag,
With Hero's "To the Rockies or BUST".

– 2 –

The scene is changed at Plymouth,
Our heroes now Behold, alas past,
With downcast eyes and deep drawn
Their tears they scarce with hold.

The man stern stolen the night before,
The ox cart lost a wheel,
The Graham's flour all run out,
Their olives all down at heel –

But still that gallant flag waves on,
Tho torn and grimed with dust,
And all that's left of its scornful brave
Is a single word just BUST.

BUST

1

Now hark all ye who list to hear our noble England's praise
And of the noble things her sons have done
In these mad modern days.

***

When two rash youths of money flush
And full of courage rare
From Portage started with gladsome heart
And never a thought or care.

***

A half starved ox these youths had bought
An ox cart made of wood
Two pairs of shoes – just one clean shirt
And Graham flour for food.

***

Oh! Gaily, gaily walk they now
Their footsteps scour the dust
And proudly waves the verdant flag
With Here's 'To the Rockies or BUST.'

2

The scene is changed, one month has past
Our heroes now behold
With downcast eyes and deep-drawn sighs
Their tears they scarce withhold.

***

The lean steer stolen the night before,
The oxcart lost a wheel
The Graham flour all run out
Their shoes all down at heel.

***

But still that gallant flag waves on,
Tho' torn and grimed with dust
And all that's left of its scornful boast
Is a simple word just BUST.

Mr Soulter's poetic prophecy was eventually to come true, but not before their trek had lasted for a month and half and taken them as far as Battleford.

We left Portage la Prairie on the 16th. June and arrived at Battleford on August 2nd. We took our time averaging about 16 miles a day, longest day being about 21 and shortest down to 6, depending on the trail and the weather. We would start away about 6.30, go on to 11.00, lie off until about 3.00 and then on till about 5.30. There was scattered settlement along all the way to Fort Ellice and some future towns were springing up. The trail was just a series of ruts across the prairie, it being the custom when one track was worn down to deep holes and roughness, a new one would be started alongside. These were the old freighters' tracks, with their Red River wheel carts connecting up the camping places on the original trails. Cultivation had in many places necessitated diverting the trail which meant going around two sides of a square instead of diagonally across it, thereby lengthening the journey.

After passing Fort Ellice the only diversions we had were those to avoid swamps and rough places. In general, travelling except when it rained was dry under foot. Nevertheless we had our fair share of swamps and sloughs to wade through. Occasionally, 'twas an all day job getting through them with water up to your waist. We stuck in one big swamp called the Wolverine, and were contemplating unloading and carrying our stuff back to high ground in preparation to getting the cart out, not looking forward to the job, when some freighters came along and put on one of their oxen to yank us out. No end of a help. Crossing some of the rivers and valleys gave us plenty to do, down one side holding the cart back to prevent it being damaged by tree stumps, and crawling up the other. We turned over one day, and sustained some damage but 'twas put to rights without much difficulty.

Some of the country we passed through was almost English Park land to look at with lakes, trees in clumps and rolling land, whilst other parts were treeless prairies with not enough firewood to boil the kettle. For fuel we gathered dried buffalo chips (dung). *Very hot at times and we had to lay up for a longer spell in the afternoon. Some pretty severe thunderstorms, rather startling at times but we pulled through without any difficulties, though one day we might have been stranded through the ox wandering off in the evening. Luckily Dalamain found it before it had gone far. Had he not done so, our journey would have been finished, for there was no way of replacing the animal and if there had been we had no money to do so.*

Day followed day with little change, often meeting no one and seeing no livestock beyond gophers, a sort of burrowing squirrel which were very plentiful. Of animals we met one bear. This was near the Indian Reservation at Touchwood some 150 miles east of Fort Ellice. Of the buffaloes that once wandered in their thousands, only their skeletons and their paths leading to water holes were in evidence, though report said there were still a few herds there. Of birds – duck, teal, prairie chicken and quail were most in evidence, and rabbits, or really hares as they don't burrow.

The curse of the country was the mosquito pest. At night and on dull days when there was no wind, there appeared no end to them. They would cover the poor old ox's back like a blanket, and one of us always walked close alongside him and fanned them off from time to time. At night we always lit a smudge fire giving out plenty of smoke. Without this nothing would have held him. He would stand feeding in the lee of it, gradually extending his distance and then when the 'squitos began work, he would rush back to the fire and bury himself in the smoke. Often at night we got little sleep, for we had no mosquito nets and had to rely on putting our heads under the blanket, which was all very well but a bit warm and required coming to the surface for a breather and then the mosquitoes made up for lost time. I have had full experience of 'squitos since then in Siam, but for attacks in mass formation the Canadian variety leave all others miles beyond.

Sundays we always laid up, did our washing and if near a decent lake or pond took a bathe. Don't know that we particularly wanted rest, but the ox did. We struck the Saskatchewan river main branch on the 28th. and from then on we went through some fine country, well timbered and watered and a treat after several days of treeless prairie, reaching Battleford on the 2nd August.

Although my grandfather had been primarily concerned with recording the daily details of their trek, it is his mention of the buffalo skeletons and their deserted trails that places him at a poignant historical moment – the end of the Indian way of life that had existed in America and Canada for thousands of years.

For the buffalo had provided the essentials of existence for the Indian. The meat was food, the sinews and bone were used for tools and the hides for clothing and shelter. But the free-running herds had become incompatible with the expanding settlements and homesteads, which is why grandfather and Dalamain had frequently to skirt round the fenced off properties rather than take the direct line. The modern world was replacing the old, and one of the major factors accelerating this change was the expansion of the railways on which my grandfather was later to work.

It was at this stage that grandfather decided to stay in Battleford as he was running out of money and there was a chance of getting some work on a farm in the neighbourhood.

The farm that grandfather now started work on was at the foot of the Eagle hills near an Indian reservation a few miles south of Battleford and belonged to an old Irishman named Boyle, who had left Ireland as a child and crossed the continent with his parents in the '49 gold rush days. Boyle had taken up one of the government sponsored homestead schemes.

He had the usual one room log house, about thirty acres under cultivation, oats and wheat, with twenty-three head of cattle. Crops averaged 25 to 30 bushels an acre. The household consisted of Boyle and his half-breed wife, her brother and another half-breed who slept on the floor and myself, who on asking where I should put down my blankets, was told anywhere you like. So as the roomiest place was at the foot of the Boyle's bedstead, I put them on the floor there and found sleeping on the floor my first experience of many such to follow. Very comfortable, and better than many of the lumpy mattresses you get in second class hotels. The floor is hard, eased a bit by the buffalo robe, but once you have got into the knack of fitting your limbs into a position conformable with it, it's all you want, and anyway hard work is a fine softener.

My work (rising about sunrise to do it), consisted of pitching the hay onto a wagon drawn by two oxen, hauling it to the barracks of the Mounted Police and then pitching it off. Ox or bull driving was an experience most aggravating, made more so I suppose by not understanding them. Leave them alone to go their own pace with plenty of "Haw, haws" and some swearing, they are all right. But they won't be hurried. Of my pair, one walked fairly fast and the other very slow. 'Twas no use cussing the cattle, so I eventually fixed up the hay fork in such a position that when he unduly lagged, he would back against the fork and a touch of the points would advise him 'twere wiser to keep up with the faster walker.

As Boyle's homestead was close to the Indian reservation, grandfather often passed Indians on the trail going to and fro from Battleford to the reserve.

I noticed the squaws would always be loaded up with whatever they were transporting, and the braves walking majestically alongside, carrying a gun if they possessed one. In some cases, the stock would be covered with round-headed brass nails, each nail said to represent an enemy killed. Some of 'em had a nice little dog. I would often see dogs used for transport with two long poles resting on a saddle on the dog's back, the ends being spread out and dragging on the ground. Between the dog and the ends, a small platform was made which carried light goods.

At the end of November 1882, work with Boyle finished and grandfather got lodgings with a man called Parker and his two brothers.

The four of us lived in the one roomed house and took shares to do the cooking , bacon for breakfast and stew for the other meals. Kept a pot on the stove into which we threw Prairie chicken, rabbits and anything of that sort that came along, mixed with bits of pork and dough balls, it made a very tasty dish. Our larder for the game we shot was a few boards under the roof where everything we shot was hung up, and in spite of the stove beneath it was promptly frozen solid. 'Twas a cold house and when the wind was blowing it meant huddling round the stove or turning in on the floor, where our blankets were spread. The house would not have been so cold had the spaces between the logs been properly done and made windproof, instead of which through the use of bad material and bad workmanship cracks appeared. Certainly we packed them up with snow, but in spite of the temperature being below zero, it could be quite warm inside and melt it. We spent our time cutting firewood for sale, shooting, using snow shoes for getting over the ground. A bit tiring at first but once you had the knack, a very easy way of getting through the snow, though hard on the first man who had to make the track.

We went into Battleford when the evenings were suitable. There were two saloons there, one having a billiard table. Liquor was not allowed, but they made a concoction of hops and sugar for which ten cents a glass was charged – dear at half the price. There was no nip in it and it would not have sold but for the fact you wanted to imagine you were having a beer. Some men would drink anything that would give a bite, eau de cologne and other scents and a favourite one was Perry Davis Pain Killer, which with hot water and sugar warmed you up quite lively. I remember in the Hudson Bay Store, a Mounted Policeman came in and asked McKay, the factor, for a drink of some kind. 'All sold out', said McKay, 'but I have a sample bottle or two of some stuff called Zozodent' (if I remember rightly). 'Twas a liquid tooth wash. 'You might try it and maybe get a bite out of it.' The MP took it away in his pocket. It was said that they would make a concoction of tobacco juice, sugar and drink that hot. I never tried it, added my grandfather, *but when the occasional permit for whisky came in 'twas enough for me.*

As there was little prospect of regular employment in Battleford, my grandfather was lucky enough to get a job with a survey party, headed by a man called Ellis, starting in March 1883. Ellis wanted someone to do the chaining[2] and keep the field book, which my grandfather, with his architect's training, was able to do. The survey was to take place in the Eagle Hills district, dividing the land into square townships, each comprising thirty-six sections of six hundred and forty acres.

We started work with the snow on the ground and used snow shoes. Ellis would set out the line, going ahead with the transit[3] and a couple of pole men and two of us would follow on behind, one dragging the front end of the chain and myself looking after the back end and keeping the field book. Not that there was much to note down beyond description of the country, water courses and such like. At every half mile, we planted a post and built a triangle of earth around it. The top of the post was marked with the number of the Section Township scratched deeply into it. They were all made to measure and of the same type, so could be found easily. The mark of our footsteps or snow shoes would leave a trail as straight as an arrow and away as far as you could see.

When, eventually, the snow started to melt, Ellis wanted the sledges that they had been using returned to a small settlement near Prince Albert called Carlton and carts brought back. Grandfather volunteered along with two other members of the party – Hynes, an Irishman and Jim Suave, a half-breed French Canadian. While at Carlton, they went to stay with Jim Suave at his parents' house.

The usual one room log cabin, with the usual stove. There was a bed in one corner where the old man and his wife slept, another in the far opposite corner, which as his two brothers slept on the floor and Hynes and myself did likewise, we wondered who it was reserved for. We soon knew for Jim said, 'Boys, I am going to get married,' which he did next day.

It took place at the small R.C. church, a wooden shack. There was a crowd of half-breeds and some Indians, who rode up on their ponies and out to make the most of it. After the ceremony, we retired to the house for a breakfast. The usual pork and beans and some tinned stuff, together with a tasty cake, made of currants, flavoured and sweetened with molasses. After this was over, dancing started and was kept up well on in the evening. The drink was Perry Davis Pain Killer with hot water and sugar and on which they got quite merry. It ran out early in the evening and so as not to stop the dance too early a collection went round and a further stock bought. They certainly enjoyed themselves.

When 'twas over and time to turn in, Hynes and I, having some little modesty or what you like to call it, suggested we should stay in the shed outside for the night. 'Oh, no!' said Jim, 'sleep where you did last night. That's all right.' So we retired, the parents in one corner, Jim and his new wife in the diagonally opposite one, the two brothers on the floor one side, and we two on the floor opposite. The next morning, the wife got up and did the household work as if she had done it daily and the following day we left and Jim left his wife behind him.

Having returned from Carlton, the survey work took them close to the Indian settlement in the Eagle Hills.

Crees, Stoneys and I think other tribes in the charge of a government agent named Payne. His duty was to teach them farming, supply stores and generally father them. There was an old chief of the Stoney tribe by name of Mosquito who used to visit us in camp, an old wrinkled man with little on beyond his Indian leggings, a vest and his robe, sometimes buffalo but more often a blanket which latter is their main garment and is always with them. He would come in and sit down and talk through the half-breed interpreter. Often whilst doing so, he would be feeling around his body and eventually between his finger and thumb he would pull out and hold up to the light a body louse, which if up to expectations he would eat, and if not put it back to fatten up.

Chief Mosquito's penchant for body lice was not the only thing that grandfather noticed about him.

He carried a round tin case about eighteen inches long which contained his treaty with the great Queen Mother and of this he was very proud and frequently held forth on it. He also carried a stick about three foot long, which contained a number of notches. The half-breed interpreter tried for a long time to get from him what these notches meant and one night when we had given him a little more tobacco than usual, he told us that these notches represented an insult from Payne. For each insult, one notch and he intended when he had reached a certain number to kill Payne. We wondered and asked him how many notches before he acted. No saying to this but 'so many notches, I kill Payne.'

Well, I suppose but for the North-West rebellion[4] which took place some two years later, he would have gone on cutting notches until he died. But this gave him his opportunity. When the rebellion broke out, the Commander at the Barracks sent word for him (Payne) to come in. This he refused to do, saying his tribes would not rise. But when a few days after, a detachment of police went to his reservation to bring him in, they found the Indians gone on the warpath and only Payne's body, which had been badly tortured. All this I heard afterwards, for I had left the neighbourhood and was in Ontario.

Besides meeting the old chief, grandfather was also present at a big Indian pow-wow in the Eagle Hills settlement.

Some hundreds of them of different tribes. They camped around a circular enclosure, built of posts and branches with a big pole through a brass ring in the centre, on the top of which was a forked seat and from which hung several lariats. In the making of braves, some would sit on top of the pole for three days, exposed to the weather and mosquitoes. Pretty bad too. Others would push a stick through the fleshy part of the chest just above the nipple and tying the end of the lariat to it would dance around until they broke the rope or pulled the stick from the flesh.

A big fire burned in the enclosure, and around this would walk the old braves, each carrying a bundle of sticks and reciting their deeds. After each recital one or more sticks – according to the importance of the deed – would be flung on the fire. After one of these, one brave flung on the whole bundle, and on asking our interpreter why so many, he said 'twas a big battle in the old days when they beat the white man. A lot of young squaws sat in one corner, singing and dancing too. An interesting night and one of the last pow-wows 'twas said would be held here.

A last contribution from Chief Mosquito ends grandfather's reminiscences of the Indians at Eagle Hills.

Old Mosquito, the Stoney Chief, got to judging our ages one day from the state of the skin on the back of the hand. Said when you could pinch it up into ridges and they stayed until you closed your hand and so stretched them out, 'twas a sign of an old man, which reminds me of a Siamese countryman judging our ages by the state of our teeth. Pitched on one of us who wore false ones as the youngest of the party. Such white and sound teeth!

In June 1883, work on Ellis' survey party finished and grandfather was paid off. But with little other prospect of work, he decided to stay with Ellis who was returning to Toronto. At Toronto, grandfather contacted his old firm of Darling and Curry for work, but with no luck. However, the latter gave him an introduction to the chief engineer of the Ontario & Quebec Railway, a man by the name of Lumsden, who got him a job as rodman[5] on the construction side of the railway based at Markham, Ontario on a salary of $45 dollars a month.

This, wrote my grandfather of what was to be his lifetime's career, *might be considered my first experience of railway work, though as an apprentice with Herbert Baker of Bristol, I did do a bit in training for the Clifton Down railway station. But of instrument work, level and theodolite, I knew little and that only of the first instrument. The latter I studied with the instrument before me in the office, and learnt sufficient of it to run a straight line and curves. My work in the field was to hold the rod and the end of the tape and in the office to work out calculations of one sort and another, plans, etc. And this was really the only training I had as an engineer. Picked it up as I went along and I suppose taking the opportunities offered. Landed me at the top after many years in Siam.*

At the beginning of 1884, work finished at Markham, but on making enquiries he managed to find employment at Sudbury with the Canadian Pacific Railway Company, who were busy extending the railway line westwards towards the Rockies. And it was with the C.P.R. that grandfather gained the practical experience that was to serve him well when he was later involved in the construction of railways in Siam.

As the company was advanced payment by the Government on the number of rails laid, work had to press on. The problem was that much of the ground consisted of swamps that had to be bridged by building banks on which the rails were laid. Then when the spring came, much of the bank work sank out of sight and had to be rebuilt by crosslogging.

This consisted of laying logs side by side the full length of the bank and putting the earth on top as a sort of floating construction. As it slowly sank, more earth was piled on and eventually a good road bed obtained. These swamps had to be crossed slowly on foot, stepping from tuft to tuft of matted grass. If you stepped between, you might go out of sight, after the manner of a Dartmoor bog.

Working conditions were very tough.

The frost in the winter would penetrate several feet in the ground, which with a temperature which would go to 40 degrees below was only natural in January. In that month in 1885, the thermometer registered from 40 degrees below to 8 degrees above, and this above zero for one day only. For twelve days, not consecutively, it ranged from 30 to 40 degrees. 'Twas cold standing about and the metal of the instruments was so cold that if your tongue touched it, as mine did one day, it stuck to it.

I remember getting badly frozen in the feet one day. Thinking it would be better with an extra pair of socks, I put 'em on, but 'twas a mistake for it filled the moccasin too tight and did not help the circulation. It took a long time to rub the frost out with snow in the usual way. We wore moccasins made of soft hide a little thicker than chamois leather throughout the winter. No soles, just the shoe like a soft glove without any additional leather for the sole. Very comfortable until the thaw commenced and then it was back to boots.

The line went all the way through bush country, large forests of pines, birch and scrub, intercepted with lakes. The timber was cut for bridges mostly in twelve inch squares and dressed on the spot with the broad axe. All the bridges were then of wood so as to push the rail work forward. They were replaced afterwards with masonry and steel, but 'twas many years before this was completed.

As work on the construction of the railway was continually moving along, there were no permanent sleeping quarters, just tents.

Our quarters, though canvas tents, were comfortable and warm in the winter as long as the small stove was burning. We pitched the tent of about 12' x 10' on a frame of logs which raised it some four feet above ground and gave about six feet of headroom at the sides. Over the tent on an independent ridge pole, the fly was spread and this kept the snow from pitching on the tent. The logs were banked up with snow and this made the tent a very comfortable place. Inside, we had a kerosene tin for a stove with a three inch smoke pipe through the tent and fly, the canvas having a tin plate, or piece of tin, let in to keep the hot pipe free of the canvas. Two raised beds made from stakes driven into the ground with a platform of small round logs on top, covered with small balsam boughs, over which was spread a buffalo robe, made a comfortable sleeping place. Always went to bed in our clothes, wearing jackets and boots and with three or four blankets on top we were quite warm. In the winter we slept with our heads under the blankets and would often wake up in the morning with the outside blanket frozen, due to our breathing oozing through the blankets and freezing when it came into contact with the cold air.... Our washing was of the scantiest and I don't remember having a bath until the spring or summer came round and I could get a swim in a lake, river or pond....

To his description of life on line in Canada, he adds (in contrast to what he would experience later in Siam) that *there was little sickness on the line. Too cold in the winter to think of it and too busy in summer.*

It is at this point that my grandfather's memoirs of his time in Canada come to an end, although he stayed on in Canada for another two years working on the C.P.R. before returning to England in 1885. One might have expected him at this stage of his life to settle down. And for a while he did, returning to the architect's practice with whom he had been apprenticed in his home area of Clifton. A career as an architect seemed to be in prospect, but the intervening years had changed him. Canada had been his initiation into adventure and three years after his return, when the opportunity came, he set off again, but this time to the other side of the world – Siam.

Notes

1. The 'old trail' (or Carlton trail) was the main transport route running from Fort Garry (Winnipeg) to Fort Carlton (on the North Saskatchewan river) and on to Fort Edmonton (now Edmonton, Alberta). The trail was used mainly by traders with their teams of Red River carts, a large two-wheeled cart made entirely of wood and hide and therefore easy to repair.

2. Chaining – a surveyor's system of measuring distances.

3. Transit-theodolite – instrument used in surveying.

4. The North-West rebellion in 1885 was a rehash of the Red River rebellion of 1869-70. Both rebellions stemmed from the native Indians' resentment at the loss of their life style and ancestral lands to settlers and other interested parties. Although the rebellions were put down, feelings of bitterness were to linger on.

5. Rodman – a surveyor's assistant who holds the levelling rod.

Old World meets the New.

CHAPTER THREE
Colleagues & Customs

In September 1893, my grandfather had finished his recuperation in Hong Kong and was back in Bangkok and calling in at the offices of the R.R.D. where Karl Bethge wanted him to start pegging out the old line from km. 170 and work through to Khorat. *More hard work and roughing it was* grandfather's immediate thought and in spite of Dr. Hayes' warning that he should not return to that area of Siam, he agreed to start on the 1st. October. Until then, he filled in time in Bangkok. *Much as usual here. Club in the evening and loafing all day. An American gunboat called the 'Concord' anchored off the bar¹ and the officers came up and had a singsong at the club.*

Oct. 3rd. Left Bangkok at 9.45 am on board a steam launch. Meant to start at 8.0 but was kept waiting an hour and three quarters for Deans. The latter (whom grandfather had already summed up as a waster) had been assigned along with an Italian, together with two fox terriers. *After 'cussing' Deans considerably, set off for Ayutthaya which we reached that evening, staying with MacGlashan.*

The next day, after picking up another assistant, a Siamese called Chitr *(the only decent assistant I ever had)*, they left Ayutthaya. *Encountered very high water and strong currents. Steering gear broke turning a sharp corner and we ran into a floating house. Smashed up the stage. Gave the johnnie 10 tics for compensation which satisfied him.*

On the 5th. October, they had reached Kaeng Khoi, where the steam launch was sent back as the rest of the journey would be on foot. But at Kaeng Khoi there was more trouble with Deans.

Deans got drunk this evening and raised a row. He would not let the Italian who shared the tent with him to sleep there. So I transferred the descendant of the Romans (and a poor one at that or he would have punched his head in) to Chitr's tent. Told Deans I would pack him back to Bangkok in the morning. But the warning seems to have had no effect, as the next day Deans was drunk again. *So put all his stuff, with the exception of some stores he bought on credit into a boat and himself along with it. He was too drunk to know anything about it.*

The boat was sent back to Pak Preo with a letter to Luis Weiler, the German Section Engineer, to pack Deans on down to Bangkok. *Well rid of him,* was grandfather's final comment.

Sunday 8th October. Left with 9 bullocks and 20 men, Chitr and the Roman to come on later with stores, etc. Reached Hinlap at 2.30 pm in a drenching rain storm, wet through (the same old game). Water running in the Hinlap creek and the trail very bad.

The day after, he left on an inspection of the line and met up with the German contingent who were working on the line at Muak Lek.

Kaeppler, Bock and Werner living in one large house. Kaeppler hardly ever leaves the house and very seldom his room for any length of time. He looks very sick and apparently spends his time in doing nothing and drinking beer. They tell me he never goes on the line and that the two assistants are doing all the work. They have finished up to km.154 and followed our old line exactly. Saw Kaeppler for about five minutes. He looks very bad. Maybe if he drank less beer and did a little work, he would be better. He twaddled on as usual. A most useless piece of humanity. Rain in afternoon.

Oct.10. Kept awake nearly all last night by Kaeppler who gets up at regular intervals to thrash a poor brute of a dog he has tied up to the verandah. My opinion of the man is that he's mad. Left at 8.30 am. No sign of the great Kaeppler. Reached a half-finished house at km. 159 at 10.15. Sent men back to Muak Lek for remainder of outfit. Heavy rain in afternoon. Damned miserable weather.

The next day, he accompanied the men taking the tents on to km.164 and then left them there to pitch them while he returned to the previous night's camp.

Camp site.

Trail fearful and the mud beyond all explanation. Drenched through as usual. Got back to camp at 3.30. Tired out. It is at this point that he succumbs to a rare moment of self-pity. *Raining cats and dogs and a most miserable look out. All alone and only the coolies and two fox-terriers for company.* But he cheers up a day or so later, when he finds a deer that had been killed by a tiger the night before. *Managed to get a fine cut off the hind quarters which he had not disturbed.*

The next month, November, the weather improved and he was able to push on, but the work was taking its toll.

The old cook got sick and died on the 22nd. at 4.30 pm. Buried him at 5.30 pm in a grave not more than 9 inches deep. Put a lot of sticks, etc. on him to prevent the animals scratching and covered him over with earth. The natives don't treat the dead very gently, just jumbled him in like a bag of old bones (which he was). Fever and too much opium smoking carried him off. He looked sixty but was only forty-four. This makes the fourth cook I have lost in this country.

A lot of men die on the trail here on their way with the bullock trains and I am afraid I was the unconscious agent of hastening one poor fellow's death. I had started a fire after leaving work to burn down the grass and it seems there was one of these unfortunates lying on the trail close by and had been lying for several days with bad fever, people passing him by every day and a village within two hundred yards. But no one assisted him or took any notice, except probably to laugh. It seems a common thing here that if a man is unable to move along to let him stay until he can or dies. The next morning when we returned, the men found him dead, with his head and one hand and his few clothes burnt. Apparently he was too weak to move , but I am inclined to think and hope that he was dead before the fire reached him, as if he had rolled over a distance of five yards he would have been out of the fire. Found another dead body on the 23rd. Just left behind by the bullock trains. Don't think much of human life out here. But it was not only the Chinese coolies that succumbed. *Kaeppler died this month and was buried at Pak Preo. Deans, the man I sent down from Kaeng Khoi, also died, and a Swedish interpreter of Campbell's. Fever and dysentery were the causes.*

Christmas 1893 was a solitary affair. *Spent Christmas in camp. Worked all day and had a solitary dinner like many more I have had. Christmas alone is a farce.* And although he had just recently received a letter from Karl

Bethge thanking him for the good progress made, it was a letter and two photos of Di Wansbrough, whom he had known back home in Clifton, which *got me longing and makes me feel discontented with the loneliness of life out here. Made up my mind to get married before another year is out..... but as a rule, anything you want never comes off just at the right moment.*

The beginning of 1894 saw grandfather in the north-eastern part of Siam, having been requested by Bethge to carry on the survey to Nong Khai. *Three hundred and sixty-four kilometres,* noted grandfather, *and wanted it done in twelve months. Like his cheek!* He added. In fact he did it in four. Such was the speed with which he accomplished the initial survey that he had some spare time in which to pay his respects to the local dignitaries, including an old Laos chief, *who had been blessed with eighty-four children, forty-two of whom are living.*

The most important visit was to Prince Prachak, brother to the king and Chief Commissioner of the province. Before the altercation with the French in the previous year, the Prince had had his headquarters in Nong Khai on the Mekong River, but as the other side of the river had now been claimed by the French, he had moved back some fifty odd kilometres to Udon Thani. Not that there seemed to be any danger of French infiltration according to grandfather's observations.

The other side of the river is now French territory but they have no one in charge, so the people have a free hand. No taxation and no laws, which they don't fail to take advantage of – free spirits, opium, etc., the former costing just one half what it does on this side. Prince Prachak was pleasant and agreeable. He is great on astronomy and very fond of manufacturing a lot of stuff of various kinds from the materials in the country, sealing wax, soap, a very good liquor made from pineapple, butter, cheese and many other things. Altogether, he seems a genius, but rather to my surprise he got talking about religion and said he believed in nothing. The only two things that he knew were true being a straight line and a circle.

A year earlier, H.Warington Smyth, an English mining engineer had undertaken an expedition on behalf of the Siamese Government to investigate a deposit of gems discovered on the left bank of the Mekong river. He too, had met Prince Prachak and witnessed his attempts to encourage the local people into trades. 'Prince Prachak is a reformer. He is very keen in reforming the Laos, but is grieved to find that they don't want to be reformed. He says, which is very true, that their work is always desultory (one month they plant rice, another they go fishing, another they wash gold in the sands) and that they will not settle down into trades. They prefer, too, to play music on their kans (reed mouth-organs) in the evenings to doing more useful things, and are, in fact, lazy.' Not surprisingly, he also found the Prince a keen advocate for a railway from Khorat all the way to Nong Khai to improve communications and modernize the territory.

Meanwhile, grandfather seems to have enjoyed a more social life for a change. Besides being presented with a pair of elephant tusks, he dined out with the Prince's entourage, together with a Captain of the Siamese army and his German wife, an Interpreter and the Secretary. The contrast with the privations of his life on the line made him note down appreciatively the bill of fare:

Macaroni soup. Tshohn fish. Baked fowl and bamboo root. Pork, potatoes and carrots. Roast duck & pumpkin. Sausage and green peas. Roast pigeons and het tan Rei. Salad. Laos macaroni. Rice curry. Dessert. Jelly & milk wafer.

He had time also to write up his impressions of the local countryside, the people and their customs.

Country all round here seems pretty good, but poorly populated. Infant mortality is great, very large numbers dying from smallpox and worms, fever and other complaints. When smallpox breaks out in a village, they all leave it at the first sign and the unfortunate patient must drag along the best way he can.

Local remedies for both human and animal complaints caught his attention as in the case of a man who fell off a ladder.

He either sprained or dislocated his foot. As nothing seemed to cure it, one of the men has taken to charm it. That is to say that he gets cold water and after muttering some incantations, takes a mouthful and squirts it on the foot, another muttering and another mouthful until the cup is emptied. Whether it's the cold water or a matter of time, I don't know, but the foot is getting better. They have strange notions. If a bullock goes lame, after checking the hoof, they examine the teeth as they tell me that if the animal gets a piece of grass between the teeth he always goes lame. A good bullock seems to be judged not so much by its size and general appearance as in various little ways in which the hair grows and in his markings. And the same with horses. I bought a pony that they decided was good in all respects. But a small, twisted tuft of hair under the neck indicated that he would not live long. They have two remedies when a horse has wind or gripes. The one is to hold a burning rag in front of his nose, which they say drives the wind out and the other is to ride him hard for a bit.

The people here are very conservative and strongly object to any innovations. Their invariable answer is that their fathers and grandfathers always did it this way, consequently it's good enough for them. Suggest the most simple improvement to them and one that they can see and admit would be an advantage, but you get the same shake of the head and 'my father didn't do it.....'

On his way back to Khorat from Nong Khai, he stopped off at Chonnabot, where he was invited to the wedding of a Laos girl.

A very simple affair. 'Twas a sort of second wedding, the first having taken place at the house of the man's father some two days previously. This one occurred at the house of the girl's parents. The girl and fellow sat in the centre of the room with their forefingers resting on a bowl containing various eatables, with the two old men, their respective fathers, sitting opposite. One of the old men droned out a long speech to the girl and the other did likewise to the fellow, lasting some fifteen minutes. After this was over, each old man took a piece of string and passing it several times across the hand of the girl, the other old man doing likewise to the fellow, told all the evil devils to leave and then flinging away the string, flung all bad luck from the couple. Then taking another piece of string and passing it across each of their hands as before, tied it firmly around the wrist, at the same time requesting the lucky spirits and gods to take possession and abide with them. The long speech to commence with I found was a sort of list of the girl's duties towards her husband and vice versa. But the girl, I noticed, had the hardest times portioned out to her as from what she had to do, she was little better than a slave. But they seem to thrive on it and grow fat. After the ceremony, the feeding commenced, but I did not stay for that. I gave 'em five tics for a present and they gave me a sarong and pillow in return.

At Khorat, he dined with the Commissioner, Phya Prasidt, whom he describes as *a very nice man, in fact one of the best I have met and seems anxious for the country to go ahead. But that last is a pretty hard matter in a place where nine out of ten of the heads would prefer to see it remain as it is. Opening up means exposing their many little ways of obtaining money from the people and would bring to light many peculiar little ways that would have to be stopped.*

But 'opening up' was exactly what the construction of a railway system was about to achieve, not only by making the corrupt local administrations more accountable to a centralized government in Bangkok, but in the establishment of quicker and more reliable communications. In his observations of life in and around Nong Khai province, grandfather had noted that local products, such as hand-woven cloth, gum collected from trees and animal skins were sent down to Khorat by bullock cart. *A journey running from sixteen to thirty days, depending on the weather, as for some three or four months from August to November, the trail is very wet and in many parts the water is up to two metres deep.*

All this would change with the coming of the railways, and it was already beginning to change. At the end of 1895, he was able to make a trip from Pak Preo to Bangkok in record time, leaving at 8.30am and arriving in the capital at 6.30pm the same day. *The quickest trip I have made in this country. In the old days, by boat to Ayutthaya and steam launch to Bangkok would take three days down and five up.*

Notes

1. Bar – a vast sandbank at the mouth of the Chao Phraya obstructing the passage of large ships which had to wait for the floodtide before they could proceed.

King Chulalongkorn, Queeen and some of the royal princes. (Private Collection)

CHAPTER FOUR
ROYAL LINE OPENING &
HOME LEAVE

Back in Bangkok, grandfather was put in charge of the Ayutthaya Section as well as drawing up plans and estimates for the Nong Khai line, which he had surveyed. Christmas, this time, was a more cheerful affair than some of his previous solitary ones spent on line.

Had my Christmas dinner with Hurst and a few of his friends. Went to church in the morning. Tiffin with Stevens and then to a cricket match in the afternoon. Altogether, had a very good day and the liveliest I have spent for some years past. But the lighter mood was soon overshadowed by the death of his friend MacGlashan, with whom he had often stayed at Ayutthaya. Then, a few days later, on his way to the office, *I saw a Chinaman hanging to a tree, a case of suicide. The tree was on the main road and within twenty yards of a police station, but he was hanging there for over two hours to my knowledge before they cut him down. They have some objection to handling dead bodies if it's a case of suicide or murder. The people continued burning joss sticks around the tree for some days afterwards until someone cut it down during the night.*

On the 4th. January 1895 the Twelfth Night Ball took place.

A fancy dress affair, held at the Custom House. 'Twas going off very well when the news of the Crown Prince's death from typhoid reached there at 10.30 and put a stop to it. Crown Prince Vajirunhis was only seventeen when he died and in keeping with royal custom his body was to rest in a casket in one of the Palace wats until the grand cremation ceremony.

The cremation of any important person combined general entertainment with the ceremonial proceedings.

'The whole business,' grandfather noted of a later occasion he observed, *'is a semi-religious circus sort of an arrangement. The bodies awaiting cremation were placed in coffins covered with gold leaf, highly decorated and surrounded with flowers, raised up on a high dais under a temporary sort of temple built of bamboo and white cotton. Candles burning all around and priests chanting and praying with occasional mourners going in to have a final audience. Outside were Chinese theatres, Siamese lakhons* (dance plays) *and sundry other hawkers – a kind of all the fun of the fair.*

But after a time, he seems to have got bored with pottering round Bangkok.

Life here consists principally (when you have nothing to do) in drinking whiskies and soda. It's certainly a thirsty place and between the hours of 6.0 and 7.0 at the club there is not much time lost between drinks.

In his book, 'Bangkok in 1892', Lucien Fournereau[1] gave a rather more jaundiced description of club life. 'Sometimes we also hear the chants, the cries and the hurrahs which the English gentlemen utter in their club after having absorbed a notable volume of whiskey and soda. In order not to be outdone, the German club let itself be heard in turn: they are playing music, they sing melodies which have nothing Wagnerian at all ..... it is an infernal din which often lasts until daylight.'

The beginning of March 1895 saw him back in the Khorat district at a camp further on up the trail from Muak Lek. Here he was occupied in building a house and altering places in the old location.

The country all round is dense jungle, and though I have made a large clearing around the house, it's very dull and monotonous after a short time. The rains set in early in April and there was considerable sickness amongst the coolies, three of them dying from cholera. That disease takes a man off very quickly in this country. One man was perfectly well at 8.0am and he was dead before midday. Cholera has been very bad down the Khorat district this spring, some hundreds having been carried off. Many of the small villages have cut off all communication with the main trail and prevent anyone coming into their houses. Other villages have left their settlements altogether and gone into the bush.

Grandfather was under the weather again too.

Had a nasty touch of bilious fever for two or three days at the end of April. Temperature up to 102 and 103 degrees.

On top of this came the news of the death of his friend Smiles from dysentery. He had been in charge of a survey party and had got a chill after a heavy thunderstorm and died after several days sickness. His death seems to have hit grandfather hard.

He was a good fellow. In fact, one of the few that I have cared to meet a second time and one of the straightest men going. We came out here together in 1888 for Punchard with Mr Galway and Angier. The former got drowned off Chantaboon and Angier is knocking around somewhere in Africa. I am the only one of the original Punchard gang now left out here.

Amongst my grandfather's papers, I came across Kipling's poem 'On the Line', pasted alongside a newspaper report of Smiles' death, which although set in India was just as apposite for those who died working on the line in Siam.

Their graves are set among forgotten ways,
    By *jhil* and river-bed, by *ghaut* and plain,
A stone's throw from the labour of their days –
    Their hand, their heart, their brain.

Their names are lost – their tale of work is done,
    Each grass-grown hillock tells the story drear:-
"On Survey or Construction such an one
    Died, and was buried here."

The white mists of the forest, chill and damp,
    The sun of noonday slew them at their toil,
The Pestilence in darkness smote their camp
    Upon the rain-logged soil. etc.

jhil: a lake
ghaut: mountain range

A lull in the construction of the railway due to a delay in the completion of a bridge enabled him to get away to Hong Kong for a month's break. First stop was at Ko Sichang.

> *As far as the roads and buildings which were erected here two years ago, the place is a wreck. Houses all to pieces and the roads falling in. Parapet walls washed away, etc. Since the French occupied it, the King has not been down and report says that he has given up all idea of ever using the place as a summer residence again.*

In Hong Kong, he checked in again with Dr. Cantlie at the Peak Hospital. He was still suffering from high fevers and although a blood test elicited the comment from Dr. Cantlie that *'twas wonderfully good for Siam,* he stayed on at the Peak for the first half of his leave. Most afternoons he walked down into Town but later on started dining out. On Sunday 22nd. September, he notes: *To dinner with Landale. 5 or 6 other johnnies there. Poker afterwards*. Between the 17th. and 27th. of September, he went to the theatre five times, three of those times in the company of a Miss Caldwell. Not being one for disclosing personal information unnecessarily, grandfather is sparing in his details about her. In fact, the next couple of times, she is referred to as E.C. If he enjoyed her company (which would seem likely as he invited her three times), this was subsumed into an impersonal remark about the evening in general, as in his diary note on the 26th: *To theatre in evening with E.C. Saw 'His Excellency' and enjoyed it very much*. But in his old albums there is a photo of Miss C's two dogs (Pincher and Jessie) posed on two chairs in a garden, which would suggest that he spent some time with her other than just at the theatre.

The end of the month saw him leaving for Bangkok again, returning via Swatow and Singapore. At Swatow, they took on board over seven hundred coolies and were not allowed to leave until there had been *a great inspection and counting by both the British Consul and the Chinese authorities*. Swatow (modern Shantou) had from the middle of the nineteenth century been known somewhat euphemistically as an immigration port for poor class Chinese who had been indentured, tricked or kidnapped to work as labourers in foreign countries. Most never returned.

> *October 7th. Arrived Singapore and anchored outside the harbour limits as not allowed to go in until passed by the doctor. Two men jumped overboard and made for a sampan. One was collared and put in chains after a little rattan application to his bare body, the other one got away. A lot of these coolies are little better than bond slaves, men brought down from the interior of China in*

gangs under a head man and shipped abroad to work off some old debt contracted by himself or maybe by his parents before him. They don't seem to like the idea of Singapore as they are sent up country to the tin mines, where the climate is bad and the work is hard – so escape when they have the chance.

Back in Siam, grandfather spent the rest of 1895 on the line in the Khorat section. The next entry in his diaries is dated 24th. July 1898, having lost the previous two years diaries in a house fire. The main event in 1896 that he recalls was the ending of Murray Campbell's contract with the Siamese Government as a result of the acrimonious relationship between Campbell and Bethge. The subsequent court case dragged on until 1901 because the original contract had stipulated that any disputes were to be settled according to English Common Law. One of the consequences of the court case was that when Bethge and then the Chief Engineer Gehrts were called away to Europe to give evidence in the arbitration, grandfather stood in for them until they returned, although as he remarks rather sourly *there was no more money attached to it – so that did not benefit me very much.*

In 1897, the two events that he particularly remembers were the opening of the line from Bangkok to Ayutthaya by the King and Queen and a return trip to England on leave. In the former event, he records that *honours went flying around, of which my share consisted of the Order of the White Elephant 4th. class. Great day and great times.* In a much later memoir of this occasion, he recalls a rather more graphic version of what happened.

Bethge lined us all up to receive him (the king). We were a great assortment. Smythe 6.6 ins. down to a little German of 5ft. Some fat, some lean some in evening dress, some in morning, and some in their own particular style. One German, I remember, in a dress coat and a

Royal line opening 1897 (Bangkok-Ayutthaya). King Chulalongkorn driving a spike on the rail track. (Private Collection)

sailor tie, yellow in colour. Bethge, with great pride, introduced us, 'My Engineers, your Majesty,' to which King Chulalongkorn with a smile replied, 'What a lot,' which may have been intended for what a number, but in my opinion was meant for what an assortment.

The second event, going on leave to England, came at an appropriate moment, as for some months he had been feeling *considerably out of sorts ..... put it down to fever, exposure and bad blood with something else on top ..... and in April (1897) I left for England.* Although the long sea journey helped to mend his health, it did not make him any more charitable towards some of his fellow passengers.

Passengers good, bad and indifferent, although there was only one who was really bad and objectionable and he came on at Port Said and luckily got off at Brindisi. Unfortunately, he sat at our table and a more supercilious, annoying johnnie I never met and gave one the impression that he was a small London shopkeeper, who had recently had money left him and was going round the world to spend it. A gentleman who carefully and ostentatiously wiped his fork, knife, plate, etc. with his napkin before using them and whose ways were always annoying. There was another man at our table, a writer johnnie, who had a considerable opinion of himself, but he was not objectionable ..... I took things very quietly and slept most of the way, except when some beast of a woman would start strumming on the piano.

Arriving back in England was an emotional moment.

Landed at Plymouth I think about the 22nd. of May. I don't remember the exact date, but I do remember 'twas a glorious day and made me glad to get back. All up through the Devon country, everything green and clean and such a light green, made things look lovely and a lot of girls who were on the platform at Exeter just made you stare. It rained after passing Taunton, which took the gloss off a bit, but nevertheless 'twas a welcome change after five years sun and heat of the east. Entering into Plymouth at daybreak, I shall never forget. 'Twas glorious.

From then on, he kept most of his thoughts to himself, probably because he was in familiar surroundings that did not need recording or explaining.

Well, I am not going to scrawl down everything I did and what I saw, but it's sufficient to say that I had five weeks in London and although under the Doctor the whole time and going for sulphur baths and rubbings, managed to put in a very good time. Of course, I saw the Jubilee[2] and of course I had a good run of the theatres, but would have had more so had I been fitter. The rest of his leave was spent mainly in the West country with family and friends until it was time to return to Siam. *Felt better for the change at home, but should have liked another three months.*

King Chulalongkorn with his children during the inauguration of the Bangkok-Ayutthaya line. (Private Collection)

Notes
1. Lucien Fournereau – A French architect and art historian who visited Bangkok briefly in 1892. His views reflect the competitive colonialism of the time.
2. Jubilee - The Diamond Jubilee marked the 60th. anniversary of Queen Victoria's accession to the throne and was celebrated by a procession through London and an open-air Service of Thanksgiving outside St. Paul's Cathedral.

Section Engineers' house. Up country.

CHAPTER FIVE
Mayhem & Marriage

The first week in November found grandfather back in Bangkok and enjoying his return.

Great times at the hotel[1] and of course I fell right into them. Resolutions are no good when the thing to be avoided is right in front of you. But his celebrations were soon over and he was to spend the rest of the year and most of the next in charge of the Pak Preo Section, *principally permanent way work and finishing off the construction. Good section to be on as decent house and fairly near Bangkok.* But before signing off for the year in his diary, he adds a little postscript to the effect that Di and I *started corresponding again after two years silence – and this, I suppose, is or might be as important a fact as any.* What had caused the break, he does not say. It's possible that back in England, Di had heard exaggerated rumours about E.C. But whatever the reason, grandfather was right in saying that the resumption *might be significant.*

The new section was also adjacent to many ancient sites which he was able to visit when he had the time. Foremost amongst these was Phra Phuttabat.

The place with Buddha's footprint, a great place for the pilgrims to come and worship, especially in January, when a number of people journey thither to the so-called footprint. Might be anything, and is situated on a small rocky hill approached by innumerable steps, some sixty feet above the ground. The print is 1.9m. long and 60 cms. broad. It's said to be an impression in the rock, but it's so covered with gold leaf and rubbish that it's hard to say whether it's on the rock at all. It appeared to me to be a manufactured article. The toes are nearly all the same length and it is a long way removed from a correct model of a foot, to say nothing of the size.

If he found the measurements of the Buddha's foot far from credible, his surveyor's training also led him to wonder *why the Saint should clamber over rocks, when there is level ground at the foot.* Nor was he impressed with the *swell pagoda shaped shrine, highly decorated with the usual gold leaf and gimcracks built over the footprint.* Not one for ostentation, any excess tended to arouse his disapproval.

Back on the line, the whole of 1898 was spent on the Pak Preo – Khorat Section with occasional trips to Bangkok.

Nothing startling, nothing exciting. All things moving in an even groove. Not overburdened with company and for days and months seeing no one except the assistants on the section. Solitary times as usual. However, there was *a little excitement on the 22nd. January (1899) at midnight. A gang of armed men robbed a house just opposite my place, guns firing, women and men screaming and shouting, dogs howling, etc. And in the midst of it, the thieves got away with six hundred ticals after badly wounding two people. I thought they were coming for my place and kept watch on the verandah with a double-barrel loaded with No. 2. Not that I should have stood much chance against thirty of them, but if two charges of shot had got into their faces, I think 'twould have made some of 'em howl.* It may have been 'a little excitement', but a few days later, *some brutes murdered a contractor of mine, by name of Rodrigues. Put two shots into him whilst he was asleep and killed him outright. There have been a number of robberies around lately, so as a precaution I sent to Khorat and got four soldiers. These with the police should be sufficient to keep off anyone thievishly inclined.*

By the middle of 1899, the whole of the permanent way construction to Khorat had been finished, leaving just the rails to be laid. Grandfather then started on a survey for the northern line which would branch off from Phachi, running up through Tarua to Lopburi and then on to Paknam Pho. But after thirty kilometres, bad weather forced him back to his base at Lopburi, where he was installed in a new Section house.

The house is situated on the site of an old wat within the city ramparts or rather earth boundary walls. Close by are the ruins of Phaulkon's palace, a Greek who was here two or more centuries ago, and worked his way so well into the then Siamese king's good graces that he was made a Chow Phraya (Chief Minister). It ended, I believe, in him losing his head, but judging by the size of the ruins of his palace, he must have had a fine time while it lasted.

Grandfather might have added that there were certain similarities between Phaulkon's career and the contemporary political situation in Siam. Phaulkon had tried to counter British and Dutch influence in the region by recommending an alliance with the French, but had fallen foul of the governing party and been executed. In grandfather's time, the Siamese were fending off the French menace on their eastern borders by encouraging Britain and Germany to take up a commercial stake in the country. Eventually, in this case, it was the Germans who were to 'lose their heads' in 1917, when all their railway personnel were interned – an incident in which grandfather was to play a part.

At Lopburi, there was also trouble from robberies and assaults on the Railway employees, not to mention wild elephants that broke down the new railway banks. But there was something else that was troubling grandfather as well. In a rare passage of introspection, he notes in his diary on November 18th., *Forty-one today, and started on the fifth decade still single and still as selfish as ever.* For the next few months, he must have been mulling this situation over, because in February of the new year he makes a cryptic comment in his diary.

> *The 3rd. might turn out rather an important day and might possibly be the commencement of a new stage in my existence.* That it was a proposal of marriage would seem to have been the case as an entry recorded a little later, states, *To Singapore in May 1900 and got married there on the 11th. of that month (wish now I had done it ten years earlier). Di sailed out from England, arriving at Singapore on the 9th. We put up at the Raffles and had a very good time seeing the town, etc., principally shopping.. Put in a week there and then left for Bangkok.*

For the rest of the year, he seems to have divided his time between the Pak Preo and Lopburi sections. This would have been a fairly daunting introduction to married life for his new bride and it is not surprising to read that in March of 1901 she went off to Hong Kong *being somewhat run down and off colour.* But for a recently married couple, the separation was hard to bear. *I miss her very much,* wrote grandfather. *Shall be glad when I hear she is on her way back.*

The year 1901 also saw the culmination of the court case concerning the Siamese Government's ending of George Murray Campbell's contract to build the Khorat line and the latter's claim for compensation. As the original contract had been drawn up in England, Campbell's claim was heard in England, where the eventual outcome went in his favour and the Siamese Government was ordered to pay 3,000,000 ticals plus costs.

It's been a dirty business from the beginning, grandfather confided to his diary. *The German element have not played a straight game at all. From the beginning, they had a down on GMC, solely because with his low tender he cut the German syndicate out of it. This was never really forgiven, consequently every obstacle that could be put in his way was done so by Bethge and Gehrts. Of course, his tender was too low but so also was the German one and neither of them was within 3,000,000 tics of what the job could have been done if properly carried out. Campbell's price was 10,000,000 ticals and the German 12,500,000. If the work had been properly conducted 15,000,000 would have seen it through. Up to now, it's cost 18,000,000 ticals and there is more yet to be done, although the line* (which had followed the original Punchard survey, on which grandfather had worked) *was opened for traffic in December last. Tack the costs and award of arbitration on to this and it will be a pretty expensive line.*

As The Bangkok Times of the 17th. December 1900 remarked, 'it has been a costly work, costly in life, in money, in time and in litigation.' It had taken eight and a half years to complete the line from Bangkok to Khorat with a death toll of thirty-five Europeans and seven thousand coolies, the latter figure more like ten thousand according to grandfather. Nor, he added, were the difficulties Murray Campbell experienced in the early days to get labour and supplies fully appreciated, especially in the impenetrable jungle of the Dong Phya Fai section, an area notorious for its high malarial incidence and which H. Warington Smyth, in his 'Notes of a Journey on the Upper Mekong', published in 1895, had described as 'a practical barrier to communication, leaving out of consideration the superstition with which the forest is, with much reason owing to its fevers, regarded, and the badness of the roads within it.'

Certainly, The Bangkok Times seems to have been sympathetic to Murray Campbell and finishes its account by saying that 'the heads of the Department who have had the construction work in hand since have by no means all the credit of the successful completion of the line.'

Whatever grandfather might have thought about Bethge's part in undermining Murray Campbell's work, he seems to have been genuinely upset on hearing the news of his death from cholera.

A wire came from Bangkok saying Mrs.Bethge was dead from cholera and he was down with it and he died shortly after, though he had passed the danger line and according to the doctors would have recovered. But he kept asking for his wife and when eventually they had to tell him, he said, 'my son is dead. My wife is dead. I die too,' and turning his face to the wall, went to join them. His son had been killed in a motor accident in Switzerland shortly before. A very nice couple and he a German of the old fashioned type before Wilhelm[2] spoilt 'em.

Much later in life, grandfather wrote that he *'got on very well with Bethge, who bore no malice for our first meeting and treated me very well. Gehrts followed him, more of the Prussian, but not bad, eventually killed in the War and he followed by Weiler, who died on his way home in 1918. Bethge was the best of the lot.*

Back on the line and now based just north of Lopburi, grandfather was taking advantage of a lull in construction work to fix up the new Section house and get things ready for the return of his wife from Hong Kong.

Rails are stuck in Lopburi and not likely to be extended to this place for some time to come as there are no funds to purchase any and apparently little chance of getting any until next April. The present year's budget put in by us asked for a trifle over five million tics of which we got a little over two million and considering half of this is owing to Germany for materials supplied, there is every chance of the work being curtailed in about three months time. In fact on this section, we are already doing so and have no work in hand excepting banks and a few bridges.

This was to be the last entry of the diaries that he kept on an almost daily basis. There seems to be a gap anyway in his diary keeping as the next entries refer to 1904 and are edited extracts rather than daily accounts.

Notes
1. Hotel – This would have been the Oriental Hotel (now the Mandarin Oriental Hotel), the first hotel built in Siam when it opened in 1879.
2. Wilhelm II (1859-1941), the last German Emperor and keen advocate of German expansionism.

Paknam Pho station. (Private Collection)

CHAPTER SIX
Law & Order

The beginning of 1904 found grandfather stationed at Paknam Pho with construction work having started again. *It's evident from the little said in my diary, I must have been fully occupied and had nothing to grumble about.* But he did have quite a bit to say about the Siamese legal system, being involved himself in a court case.

May 21st. Appeared in the Court at Paknam Pho to prosecute a coolie for obtaining money under false pretences, he having had advances for his coolies, which advances he had kept himself. It's some two months since I laid the charges against him and he has been in jail ever since. This detention was entirely unnecessary as there were no witnesses to appear against him except myself. The evidence was firm and the man admitted the whole business. I expected that the judgement would be given right away and asked the presiding magistrate not to be hard upon him and told him I thought the two months imprisonment the man had already undergone was sufficient and I only wished to bring the case as an example to the other coolies. He said nothing and I left. Subsequently, I found that he had adjourned the case. A month later, the man was still awaiting sentence. He sent to me asking for my assistance in getting the matter settled, but I could do nothing. What was eventually decided I know not, but assume that a certain amount of money changed hands before 'twas finally concluded.

Back in the late 80s and early 90s, within my own recollection and experience, many a poor devil was kept in jail for a year or more and often on fake or trumped up charges. I remember in '89 talking to a prisoner who told me that he had been waiting for two years to be tried on the charge of stealing a chicken, and was just as likely or not to wait as long again unless his friends could find money.

The middle of 1904 saw a visit to the line by the new Director General, Luis Weiler and another German called Kloke.

June 24th. Weiler and Kloke turned up, the former just arrived to take over from Gehrts. Weiler was a Section Engineer on the Hinlap Section from '93 to '98 and then left. Since then he has been in China. As a Section Engineer he was not bad, but rather too finicking. Don't know how he will turn out as D.G. Anyway, don't think he will worry me (and he didn't). Pleasant as of yore. Kloke is a blatant ass, perfect in his own estimation, which is as well for him, for to others he is an egotistical, footling idiot. I see he arrived with a bad knee, got chucked from his pony. I made a note that he had better travel in a pannier for the future, himself one side and his goods the other. It's a pity he did not adopt this style of transport, for some time after when riding in Bangkok he was thrown and picked up unconscious, suffering from concussion of the brain. This so affected the small quantity he possessed that he was eventually compelled to leave the country – heart or something (possibly too much Rhine wine).

Grandfather's antipathy to some of his German colleagues was not only for personal reasons. Professional disagreements played a part too.

During the whole of 1904, I was stationed at Paknam Pho in charge of the construction, some 28kms. of that section of the Northern Railway line. I first struck the place in '88 and in company with Smiles, a good chap dead these ten years, surveyed the line from Paknam Pho to Phitsanulok. We kept near the riverbank of the Mae Nam, through low lying country liable to flooding from one to four metres deep during the rains. Had to do so to follow instructions. Reported against it and advised keeping further away to the east on the higher ground, which advice was not followed unfortunately when the permanent line was located some fourteen years after. The present location of the line is a great mistake and will be a costly piece of work to keep in order. Banks the whole way, some places up to eight metres high and for the greater part nearly four metres up to near Phichit. The floods come within a metre to the grade level, with the result that the banks are continually slipping away. Some of Gehrts' work. I told him of the mistake, but he was much too self-opinionated a man to follow anyone's ideas but his own.

Grandfather's misgivings were justified when a year later, he had to stop a train coming into Paknam Pho station.

Had to stop traffic over the bank leading into the station. It's a bank some twenty feet high and goes all to pieces during the floods, slips right away and leaves the track hanging in the air. Closed it just in time or we should have had a passenger train in the soup.

Some four years later, when the line to Phitsanulok was officially opened, the minister of Public Works, Prince Nares, referred to the difficulties and expense of the earthworks about which grandfather had warned. 'The earthworks have not been carried on without difficulty, and the expense has been high. The floods necessitated an embankment two to three metres high, with many places of six metres on the lower ground. During the rainy season, extensive slips occurred in these banks and these had to be made good ..... all this added considerably to the cost.'

September 1904 brought him the sad news from England of the death of his favourite sister, Lucy.

Poor old girl, only forty-four. She had an accident some few months previously when her dressing jacket caught fire and burnt her arms and neck. This coming on a system already weakened with years of indifferent health was too much for her and eventually carried her off. I note I quoted a verse:

All is ended now, the hopes and the fear and the sorrow,
All the aching of heart, the restless, unsatisfied longing,
All the dull, deep pain of constant anguish and patience.

I don't think, he added, *I ever felt anyone's death so much* and it was surely no coincidence that he quoted lines from Longfellow, as the poet's second wife had also died after sustaining burns from her dress catching fire.

However upset he was at the death of his sister, he had the oncoming birth of his first child to look forward to and in readiness for this event, he accompanied his wife to Bangkok at the end of December.

To Bangkok with Di. We were two nights out on the way, but having a big house boat were quite comfortable and she enjoyed the trip. Water up country was nearly at low level and the launch had not much to spare. In fact, she rubbed on some of the sandbanks. First night mosquitoes were bad and Di had neuralgia which kept her awake, but it passed off during the day. Arrived on the 23rd. and put up at Dr. Hayes in readiness for the important event.

Although grandfather returned to Paknam Pho after seeing his wife comfortably settled in under the care of Dr. Hayes, he was back in Bangkok at the beginning of February 1905 for the birth. A short note in his diary recounts what happened.

Feb. 9th. A sad day, especially for Di. Gwennie, for that would have been her name, was born dead. Di much cut up but bearing up bravely. Very sad business.

10th.. Buried the little thing in the Bangkok Cemetery at 7.30 am. Remained in Bangkok with Di, helping to cheer her up until the 21st., when I left for Paknam Pho.

Whatever else he may have felt about the loss of his first child, he kept to himself. But perhaps in an attempt to put the shock of what had happened behind him, he drove himself very hard on the return journey, taking only three days and culminating in a final day of seventy-two kilometres:

made up of twelve kilometres by train, fifty-eight riding (3 ponies) + 2 walking – the last at the end of the journey. A hard day for this country and one not often accomplished. Seldom, I should say. The riding was a good feat, because I have had little of it for the past few years and I was pretty stiff before half way through, but it wore off with the journey.

But in spite of his satisfaction in still being able to tackle the physical challenges of his job, marriage had given him a new, softer outlook on life. He found any separation to which they were subjected increasingly unwelcome and now, on her return to Paknam Pho, Di became unwell and had to retire to Si Racha on the coast where the climate was less oppressive. By the beginning of April, grandfather was becoming increasingly concerned.

April 8th. Still no Di. Wired her to come (I had ordered a travelling chair from Hong Kong). Dear thing, as anxious to get back as I am to have her. This single life is no life at all. It was to me one time, but not now. They finally met up on the 15th. and travelled back to Paknam Pho, *glad to be there together again.*

On the line, work continued slowly because May was an unusually hot month.

One of the hottest I have experienced. Max. temp. in the shade ran from ninety-four degrees to one hundred and four and min. seventy-two degrees to eighty for twenty-two days. The max. temp. one day was from one hundred degrees to one hundred and four and the heat was stifling. Very little work done. Coolies and all quite played out and small blame to 'em. Was a bit that way myself. However, he managed to complete the erection of two steel bridges on his section.

The following month he paid a visit to the jail at Paknam Pho.

The prisoners are chained heavy or light according to sentence and at night time a long chain is passed between the legs of each prisoner and fastened at each end of the building. On one occasion, however, they got the end of the chain clear and scooted out. One was under sentence of death and the others lifers. The man under sentence was recaptured and he is now chained and doubly chained with about 100 lbs. weight on him and confined in a small tiger cage with room enough to lie down in a cramped position only. When I saw him he was chained to the cage and sitting up looking damned miserable and judging from the thinness and weakness of him would hardly live long enough for his sentence to be carried out. His appearance was made worse by two wounds in his lower jaw, a rifle bullet having shattered it, fired by a policeman when recapturing him. Judging from his looks, he appeared a weak, harmless idiot and nothing like the blackguard he was said to be.

The grounds and the buildings are kept very clean and the prisoners, apart from the one in the cage, have little to complain about. Food plentiful and smoking allowed and other luxuries if provided by friends or other outsiders. They are together in groups and talk as much as they want. Work light. Road cleaning, sawing, gardening and odd jobs and beyond being chained may just as well be free. The Governors find these prisoners very useful for work around their compounds and they save them the cost of several servants.

In October, King Chulalongkorn opened a further section of the line to Paknam Pho. The Minister of Public Works first made a short speech, after which the King replied, acknowledging the great advantages that Railways were to the country and declaring the line open.

Afterwards, he walked around and spoke to two or three people of which I was one. "How long have you been here now, Mr Gittins?" And on my replying seventeen years , he commented,. "A long time." A very pleasant man with a very fine manner. He gave me the Third Class Order of the Crown, which I should have thought more of had he not given the same to two Germans of many years less service – ten and five to their credit as against my seventeen. But with a Fatherland Director, it's only natural that he should push his countrymen forward. Returned in evening to Paknam Pho and glad to be back. Don't like these ceremonies.

In November 1905, grandfather was promoted to Division Engineer by the new Director General, Luis Weiler, who had taken over from Gehrts the previous year. Weiler's promotion of grandfather (a 'Britisher') indicates the respect in which he was held, although negotiations over salary were not so amicable.

Whilst in Bangkok, had a long jaw about salary with Weiler for the new post of Division Engineer he has just given me and 'twas about time I had some promotion. Salary offered inadequate and told him so, but he would not see it. Had an interview with Prince Damrong (the

Minister of the Interior) to solicit his influence. Pleasant chat and nothing more. Affable and genial as he always is, but they don't like to interfere in the business of other departments outside their own. But he did invite grandfather on a trip down the Siamese Malay peninsula for the following year.

The rest of 1905 was involved in finishing up at Paknam Pho.

Packing, final calls, handing over ..... after three years residence, it has been very pleasant quarters and both Di and myself enjoyed it, tho' I think she found it a bit lonely at times, especially so after the loss of the child. But the return to Bangkok would have pleased her as the British constituted the largest number of Europeans there and the English Club provided a home from home. Fournereau, who was no anglophile, described the evening rituals of the Club in his customary acerbic tones. 'On the landing of the English Club, washed by the Menam (Chao Phraya), the misses and the ladies come to take fresh air, gossip in English, flirt in English, surrounded by a troop of English adorers, which whisper them sweet words in English. Beware,' he went on to say, 'of penetrating this sacred enclosure: you derange everybody and a few icy looks make you quickly feel like an intruder. ....'

The beginning of 1906 saw grandfather starting his new work to the east of Bangkok.

The line follows the track of my preliminary survey for the Bangkok – Si Racha line via Paet Riu, laid down by me in 1901-2. But the first portion, that to Paet Riu, is only to be put in hand. To reach Si Racha necessitates a big bridge across the Bang Pakong river, which is some two hundred metres wide and fourteen metres deep. An expensive work and not justified by the amount of traffic

Bangkok and Menam (Chao Phraya) river. (Private Collection)

to be expected. Time is not ripe for pushing beyond the present proposed terminus.

Work on the new line required frequent inspections. On one trip, he put up with the Section Engineer, named Altman (whom he had briefly met in 1892 , along with the Chief Engineer, Rohns). He seems to have received somewhat grudging approval. *I suppose according to his lights he is not a bad sort, but I can't cotton to the Fatherland fraternity.*

On another inspection trip, he returned by ferry launch, the "Paet Riu".

A dirty old hookah, licensed to carry thirty passengers for which there is no accommodation but the deck and a rabbit hutch of a cabin which is used by the "officers" and their women as a living place and is also given up to Chinese passengers or others who prefer to lie up in the bunks and smoke opium – and this was consumed pretty steadily judging by the smelly air that crept up the hatchway. The route taken by these boats is down the Bang Pakong river, along the head of the Gulf, passing Paknam up the river to Bangkok.

We left at 7.45pm and reached the mouth of the Bang Pakong river at midnight and dropped anchor, waiting for the tide. A choppy sea and I reckoned for a choppy time, but luckily when she swung round to her anchor, she steadied up. Stayed there, sitting and dozing in a folding chair until 3.0am when we up anchored and got away. Choppy sea and much pitching. Did not mind that much, but did growl a bit when a rain storm came on and all the awnings were let down. This bottled up the stink coming from thirty odd Chinese and in spite of nearly choking myself by endeavouring to keep out the stink with a handkerchief stuffed up my nose, it eventually turned me up for about five minutes. The stench from a gang of Chinese coolies confined in a small space, together with their belching and spitting would turn a cast iron stomach up.

After this trip, he wrote, *glad to get back again. Don't think so much of these excursions as I used to. It makes a great difference when you have snug quarters to come back to. I hustle along as much as possible to reach 'em. But when you have bachelor quarters, it does not much matter whether you are in them or not.*

This was to be the last trip he made as Division Engineer as the previous month he had been offered a new post.

Feb.26th. Called on the Minister of Public Works about a new appointment as Technical Secretary to the P.W.D. Had a long talk with him. Seems to be a decent job and only a question of pay which will apparently be all right. Said I would accept it conditionally. The post is really Technical Adviser, but they don't like the latter word as it hurts their susceptibilities, also those of the Germans and other nations, who would be jealous that another good post was given to a Britisher. We hold most of 'em as it is. Personally, given the same pay, I would rather remain in the Railway Department. More work and more interesting.

However sensitive the Siamese may have been to the role of their foreign advisers, the fact was that they played an essential part in the modernization of Siam. In King Mongkut's time and that of his successor Chulalongkorn, there were very few educated men sufficiently qualified to fill the essential administrative posts, apart from the more able members of the royal family who were often educated abroad and had travelled widely outside Siam. So the foreign advisers supplied the expertise that was badly needed. Nor were they just foisted on the Siamese by foreign governments. In nearly all cases, they were selected, appointed and paid by the Siamese Government, and although there was no obligation to follow their advice, more often than not it was. A few of the advisers were even rewarded with the title of Chao Phya, the highest non royal rank. The Siamese were careful, however, (as in all their dealings with foreign powers) to prevent any one country having too much influence by recruiting them from different countries, although grandfather was correct in saying that in 1906 the British had the biggest number.

There was another more political side to grandfather's appointment which was aired in The Times obituary (13/2/1937) and which illustrated yet again the intense rivalry between German and British interests in the Railway Department. 'Gittins was the senior Divisional Engineer and the next for appointment as Deputy Director with the Directorship to follow as a matter of course. But it was desired in the highest German quarters to make the Royal Siamese State Railways as far as possible a German enclave, and the Director now informed the Government that if a British Deputy Director was appointed, he and most of his men would resign.'

If this was the case, it would explain the offer of the new job to grandfather in the Public Works Department, where the Siamese could still benefit from his expertise, as the P.W.D. covered railways anyway, and at the same time keep the Germans happy in charge of the Railway Department. 'A diplomatic imbroglio', as The Times described it, was thus avoided.

On May 31st., there is a matter-of-fact note in grandfather's diaries that *I severed the connection with the R.R.D. after nearly eighteen years continuous service on railway work in this country and took up the duties of Technical Secretary to the P.W.D. Promotion at last.*

Along with his new job came the good news of the successful birth of his second child, John Wansbrough.

Everything, thank God, went off all right this time. But with the happy news came news of deaths. *Folkens, Chief Accountant of R.R.D. died from cholera and the next day Thiel, Head of the Central Office (Clerks) died of the same complaint. It has been a very bad season for cholera and numbers have died, some thousands of natives and Chinese and twenty or more Europeans. A long, hot, dry season. No rain and consequent scarcity of good water is the cause of it.*

Survival, as so often in grandfather's life, seems to have been a matter of lottery.

Train with inspection carriage over timber trestle bridge.

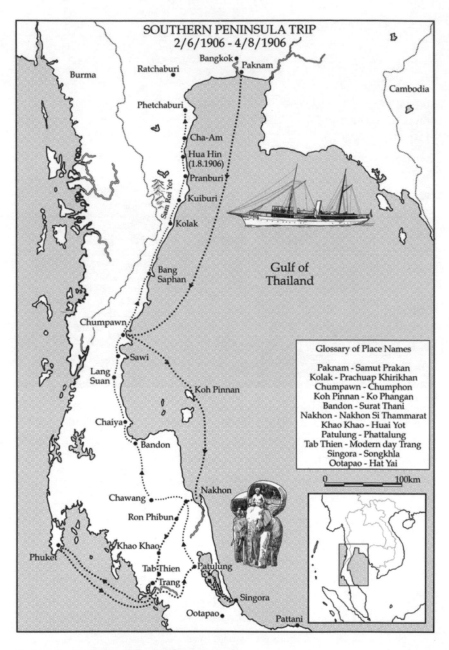

SOUTHERN PENINSULA TRIP
2/6/1906 - 4/8/1906

Burma

Ratchaburi

Bangkok • • Paknam

Cambodia

Phetchaburi

Cha-Am

Hua Hin
(1.8.1906)

Pranburi

Sam Roi Yot

Kuiburi

Kolak

Gulf of
Thailand

Bang
Saphan

Chumpawn

Sawi

Lang
Suan

Koh Pinnan

Chaiya

Bandon

Chawang

Ron Phibun

Nakhon

Khao Khao

Tab Thien

Patulung

Phuket

Trang

Singora

Ootapao

Pattani

Glossary of Place Names

Paknam - Samut Prakan
Kolak - Prachuap Khirikhan
Chumpawn - Chumphon
Koh Pinnan - Ko Phangan
Bandon - Surat Thani
Nakhon - Nakhon Si Thammarat
Khao Khao - Huai Yot
Patulung - Phattalung
Tab Thien - Modern day Trang
Singora - Songkhla
Ootapao - Hat Yai

0   100km

Sothern Peninsula Trip (2/6/1906–4/8/1906).

CHAPTER SEVEN
The Discovery of Hua Hin

In June 1906, grandfather joined Prince Damrong on the trip (to which he had been invited the previous year) down the Siamese Malay peninsula. Since 1894, when King Chulalongkorn had made him the first Minister of the Interior, Prince Damrong (who was a half-brother to the king), had been involved in the reorganization of the old, inefficient and corrupt provincial administrations into a more centralized system. By creating new administrative areas (monthons) with centrally appointed governors, he aimed to break the power of the provincial nobility with its inherent corruption and create a civil service with salaried officials responsible to central government. In this way, both taxes and justice could be more fairly and efficiently administered.

But after centuries of the old system, the new ideas were taking time to be introduced and were less easily imposed on the provinces further away from Bangkok, which made the development of a countrywide railway system all the more crucial to the success of his plans. Prince Damrong himself was constantly going on tours of inspection to monitor progress and encourage the new officials and the trip on which grandfather joined him seems to have been both an official and private visit.

2nd. June Left Bangkok by train for Paknam at 8.0am in company with Prince Damrong, his three little girls[1] and others. Also Dr. Braddock and a photographer by name of Preuss from Lenz. On reaching Paknam went on board the yacht 'Srithramarag' and up anchor about 9.0. Sea choppy and a considerable pitch and roll on. Looks as if the trip will be a pleasant one. Everyone happy.

The first major stop was at Chumpawn, where they went out to the islands where the birds' nests (the edible nests of the Chinese) are to be found.

The birds are like small swallows and build in caves. The nests are of a gelatinous substance, suspended from the walls like scallop shells and are placed very close together some ten or twelve to the square foot. The first nests built are taken and the substance is very fine and pure. This constitutes the first quality and runs in value to upwards of twice its weight in silver. These being taken, the birds build a second time, but the material this time is less pure and discoloured. It is also taken and constitutes the second quality. On building the third time, they are allowed to remain for nesting and after this is over, the stuff is collected and classed as third quality. This is dirty, mixed with feathers and other impurities and commands a comparatively small price. The birds lay two eggs and are fairly tame, which is accounted for by the fact that men are always about the caves, acting as guards to prevent thieving. They are all armed and do not hesitate to shoot any doubtful characters, especially so at night.

The islands are farmed out and constitute a considerable source of revenue to the Government. The Chinese look upon the food as strengthening and good for weak digestion. To me, it's almost tasteless and like common isinglass.

After Chumpawn, the next stop was at Koh Pinnan.

An island with a good, fresh water supply. Bathed and the crew had a good wash. Quite necessary, as they don't take kindly to salt water and so miss their daily baths on the boat. There are about one thousand people settled on the west side of the island, occupied in gardening and fishing. The fresh water runs over some shallow falls and the place is pretty.

Four days after setting off from Bangkok, the party arrived at Nakhon bay, where they had to tranship to a smaller boat which could manage the shallow off-shore waters and navigate up river to the town of Nakhon. They spent several days here, exploring the surrounding countryside in what is now the Khao Lung National Park. On the 9th. June, the expedition proper set off.

Left at 8.0am. Long caravan. Prince Damrong, his children, various retainers, Dr. Braddock, Preuss, self and officials of the district. We started away with sixty elephants, about four hundred horses, sundry ponies, etc. and made a pretty imposing circus.

Elephant transport.

In spite of his normal reticence, grandfather was obviously impressed. Fortunately for him too, he had not been involved in the logistics of the expedition, although by the end of the trip he did begin to question its expense and funding.

That first night, they camped at Ron Phibun, having covered a distance of about twenty-five kilometres from Nakhon. The next day, they visited the first of many tin mines they were to visit.

10th. June   To the mines in the morning, worked by Chinese. Very much of the British workman about one gang of Chinese coolies. They had brought their clock out from their quarters and placed it in a conspicuous position in the workings. They did not mean working one second after knocking off time.

From these tin mines, the party continued westwards, crossing the divide between the China Sea and the Indian Ocean. This also involved crossing the boundaries from Nakhon province to Phuket, where they were met by the Governor, Phya Rasada, a *very fat, short Chinaman minus his pigtail, which was cut off some time ago when he was made a Phya and became more or less Siamese.* He was the sixth son of a Chinese immigrant, Khaw Soo Cheang, who had made good and had risen to be Governor of Ranong.

Rather a wonderful man. Can't read or write. Runs his province very well both for his own and the Government's benefit ..... appears to have a hand in the steamship lines, mines, farms, etc. Said to be a millionaire in dollars several times over and I guess it's not far from the truth.

By the 12th. June, they had reached Khao Khao (modern day Huai Yot), where after inspecting more tin mines, they spent a whole day visiting some caves about eight miles to the west.

Started off in the morning, ponies and chairs. The first cave was a small one at the foot of the hill. Not much of it, but important on account of a number of clay tablets of buddhas that are buried there. They are small things, two to three inches in diameter, rather round or heart-shaped with small figures of Buddha stamped on them. They are of clay, sun-dried and buried in the ground. Said to be over one thousand years old. I am of opinion that they were originally left in heaps and have become buried over the course of centuries, partly by the decay of their own materials.

Had tiffin on the banks of a large river and then went on to some more caves. These were really interesting, situated in a limestone hill rising out of the plain. The caves, starting in at the bottom, worked their way up through crevasses to one larger cave about one hundred and fifty feet above the plain. This cave had one or two openings overlooking the plain, the view from which was rather grand, except that as it rained damned hard, we didn't see much. Should like to stay here a few days and fossick around. Started back about 3.0pm. Raining and bad going under foot.

It was at this point, that grandfather grew impatient with the slow rate of progress and struck out on his own, although he nearly came to regret his decision.

I gave up the chair and started walking ahead of the party, as their pace was too slow for mine. The trail was through the bush until it joined the main road some three quarters of a mile from camp. Got pitch dark before I was out of the wood and I did not like it. Ran against buffaloes, elephants (and though they are tame, they give one a bit of a shock when you suddenly see one looming up out of the darkness ahead of you), to say nothing of it being tiger country. Hard, wet walking. Decidedly glad when I struck the main road. Got home a full hour ahead of the others and had taken my bath and swallowed some hot tea and whisky before they turned up.

Leaving Khao Khao, the party next followed the trail south to a large settlement called Tab Thien, arriving on the 14th. *The trail for the last part of the journey went through a cultivated district, a rich country with a good future before it. Most of the province of Phuket appears to be good land and tin lies along the hills.* And with an eye for future railway plans, he added, *only wants communication.* With this in mind, he spent the next day getting information for a railway line, before they left by river launch for Trang (which at that time was situated on the coast).

At Trang, grandfather noted that it should become a decent trading town when the railways got there, providing they spent some money on improving the approach by sea, dredging the bar and river in places. (In fact, ten years later, the town was moved inland twenty-six kilometres to what was then Tab Thien and became the modern day Trang). From Trang, they crossed by boat to Phuket, after the usual transhipping manoeuvre as the coastal steamer had to lie a long way out, arriving in the early morning of the 18th. June.

Reception, of course, on landing. The usual priests, headman, officials, etc. ..... Phuket is purely a tin mining place, worked by the Chinese and I should say that it was pretty hard for anyone to compete against them. Always keen to observe and record working practices and conditions, grandfather noted that *the coolies are paid at the rate of $1 per day and their food, which costs about seventeen cents a man. They are generally on twelve month agreements and during that time their purchases from the Towkay's store for clothes, opium, tobacco, spirits, etc., run into a pretty large lump of their* *savings, with the result that when settling day comes, few of them have much money coming to them and some are overdrawn...... The tin lies in a vein about fifteen inches deep, some twenty feet below the surface and the whole of this top layer is moved by coolie labour before the tin can be worked. The whole place is gradually being turned bottom upwards.*

But besides pottering around Phuket and visiting the mines, he was busy working on a railway plan and it was at Phuket that grandfather first proposed the scheme that three years later was to come to fruition with the construction of the Southern Line.

Talking to Prince Damrong one day about railway construction southwards, I told him that the proposed scheme to simply build a few disconnected lines in Phuket and Nakhon was nonsense, and proposed to him that I should return overland from Singora to Phetchaburi and report on a line right through as that was the only correct policy if they wanted to open up the country. He thought this over for a night and the next day said he agreed and added you can do just whatever you like. I leave it to you to draw up a report as you think fit.

The next day, the party returned to Trang from Phuket and then left for the overland trail to Patulung at the northern end of the inland sea leading down to Singora, taking four days to arrive.

The inland sea is very shallow and a nasty, choppy sea gets up in a very short time and there is much pitching and tossing about of the boats. The storms don't last very long and in shallow water the men get out and hold onto the boat on either side to steady her. Here, they are standing on hard ground, but the Malays of the western coast when overtaken by a squall at sea do the same thing, with the difference that they are in deep water and swim alongside holding the sides of the boat.

At Singora, there was a fine, sandy beach and grandfather got in some good sea bathing.

Not at all a bad place for a summer residence. It's an old settlement and in the old days was often raided by Chinese pirates who apparently frequented this coast whenever they wanted a little fun and money – and a bust in general. And it was at Singora that he parted from Prince Damrong, who was going on further south to Pattani. *A very nice man is the Prince and one of the few really fit to govern his country,* he commented in his diary. *Most of them are not except in the old fashioned way of lining their own pockets first.*

So on July 1st. 1906, grandfather started his journey back to Phetchaburi, intent on the survey for a railway. Having returned to Patulung by the inland sea again, he then headed as directly north as possible to Nakhon. For the first part of the way, he was accompanied by the local amphur (local dignitary) and a dwarf *who was said to be a fortune teller or something of that ilk.*

I asked him if I was married. 'Yes.' 'Any children?' 'Yes, two.' 'Both living?' 'No, one dead.' 'Which is living, boy or girl?' 'Girl.' Here he made a mistake, but it was rather an extraordinary series of right guesses – or something.

From Nakhon, he set off for Bandon via the Khao Thong pass, having met up with the elephants which had been left behind on the journey down.

The pass is about six hundred feet high and is rather rough going – fit only for elephants and pack animals. On the west side, it drops into a good valley and open bush country, well watered along the banks of a stream from

Elephants drinking.

the hills – Khlong Di. Camped at a village of that name for the night.

His route then took him up through Chawang, pressing steadily northwards until he reached Bandon, where he arrived on the 13th. July. From then on, the route north was never far from the thin stretch of coastline, overlooked in places by the mountainous border with Burma. At Chaiya, which he reached on the 15th., his carefully planned itinerary for the following day was upset by the local amphur arriving late – an action that was guaranteed to exasperate him.

Had arranged with the amphur for an early start this morning but did not get it. He strolled along about 8.0am. Much too big a man and like most of the officials in this country utterly useless. None of them take any interest in their work beyond getting the largest possible squeeze out of everything that passes through their hands. Got away about 9.15.

The route now involved crossing several rivers which wound down from their sources in the mountains to their outlets in the sea. At Lang Suan, he found the river just passable for the elephants, but at Sawi, which he reached on the 19th., he had to camp on the banks of a river which was seventy metres wide, whilst the elephants were sent away up stream to find a crossing, the water being too deep at the normal ford. *Which difficulty,* commented grandfather, *in crossing the rivers and creeks during the rains is the curse of this country.* The arrival at Chumpawn the next day posed even more difficulties.

20th. July Arrived at Chumpawn about 3.0pm. Heavy rain previous night and the country and creeks flooded. In consequence, had to swim the elephants over two rivers and boat our baggage and selves across.

21st. July At Chumpawn all day, where he was not impressed by the local administration. *Found the Telegraph operator stretched out at full length on the office table fast asleep and the Post Master gone visiting. Had decent quarters in the Governor's house and that's all that can be said for Chumpawn.*

The next day, he continued his journey northwards, keeping close to the coastline. The weather was still bad but by the 24th. July they had reached Bang Saphan.

Past ten days were wet and dull and the going has been a bit hard. Weather makes all the difference in this sort of work, tho' come foul or come fair when you are camped up for the night and your dinner inside you, the day's discomforts are soon forgotten in sleep.

But from then on, things changed for the better. The weather improved and he was able to bathe in the sea when they set up camp at the end of the day. By the 27th. July, the party had reached Kolak.

A *small shipping place with junks and occasionally small steamers. Finished our elephant transport here after four hundred miles of that mode of conveyance. It's a good way of moving about and providing you get an easy moving elephant a very pleasant one, but some of them do sort of hump you up. From here we walked and used carts for transport. Tried riding in one of the carts but that is an experience one does not want to repeat.*

28th. July A late start, 9.40. Carts turned up early and having hung around for a bit, the drivers found they had no grub, so vamoosed to get it. On their return, 'twas discovered that the carts had no covers. So they set to and made a few to protect the bedding and such like – no system and from the governor downwards useless .....
Phetchaburi province is a nest of thieves and the villages are looted night after night – due, I think, to the Governor at Phetchaburi, who having given two daughters to the King, presumes upon it and is allowed to do what he pleases and like the governors of the old days he is the chief robber of the district. Complaints about his misgovernment everywhere, but nothing is done by the Bangkok authorities. Too much influence under the sheet and that is always bad.

Phetchaburi province aside, grandfather does acknowledge that taking the governors all round and giving them their due, they are a vast improvement on the rogues and thieves they had when I first came here. In those days, they were king of their districts and the farther away from Bangkok, the more their power was exercised. No regular accounts were ever submitted to Bangkok of the year's taxation. A sum of money was sent down and as long as this equalled the estimate submitted in the yearly budget, no enquiries were made. The Governors took good care to be always on the right side by estimating the annual amount under that which they knew they would collect and then by sending down a surplus gained kudos where none was deserved.

Prisoners, as grandfather had frequently noted, were kept in jails on trumped up charges, so that they could be employed by the governor on his own private work.

It was not a difficult matter in those days to keep the jails full. There were more innocent ones than guilty and the latter consisted principally of petty offences. – two weeks to six months in an ordinary country but here the same number of years. The governor also, or some of them, controlled the gang thieves or if they did not control them, 'twas their retainers, who never receiving any pay for their services, took to gang robbery to recoup themselves and the governor winked the other eye. The poor labourer in those days got little in the way of cash or anything else except stripes for his labour.

Back on the trail, grandfather was still cussing the province of Phetchaburi.

Only good thing about it is the sea and that is beyond the power of the Governor and his assistants to interfere with – or they would soon spoil that also. At Kuiburi, he was confronted with *a biggish stream. Had to unload carts and boat the stuff across. Have been very lucky in crossing the creeks, water for the most part being low. It would be a very different journey after heavy rains, and a hard one.* After Kuiburi, the party passed over a plain overlooked by the Sam Roi Yot range of hills and on the last day of the month reached Pranburi, *a flourishing little place by the sea but smelly like most of these places. All day here, arranging for bullock carts for tomorrow.*

On August 1st. 1906, he arrived at Hua Hin after *a soaking, heavy rain all the afternoon,* but was still sufficiently impressed by the little fishing village to note down that *it should make* a good seaside resort.[2] *Good beach and high ground.* And with that observation, grandfather set in motion a chain of events which led directly to modern day tourism in Thailand, because it was he, who some time later recommended Hua Hin to Prince Purachatra, who in turn recommended other members of the Royal family and nobles to acquire land there and build holiday homes. Prince Purachatra himself, had the Railway Hotel constructed in 1921, while in 1928, King Vajiravudh built his Klai Kangwan ('Far from Worries') palace there. But the development was only possible after a railway line had been built to connect Hua Hin with the capital and this service grandfather duly provided with his construction of the Southern Line.

But all this was in the future. In 1906, grandfather was still pushing northwards in the rain from Hua Hin, up through Cha-am and then Tha Yang before finally arriving in Phetchaburi on the afternoon of the 4th.August, where he could take the train to Bangkok.

Been a pleasant and interesting journey, he confided to his diary, *but having reached a stage when your own fireside is best, the main object on these journeys is to get back as soon as possible. Anyway, I have had enough of them in my time. I squash any desire to hanker after 'em.* This did not stop him, however, being rather pleased with himself, when having gone on ahead, he reached Phetchaburi a good eight hours before the main party arrived. *Baggage turned up at 10.0pm. I had turned in, or sort of turned in, on the table with a towel for a blanket and my coat for a pillow. Quite the old style again, but it was not as comfortable as it might be. Table too short and covering not enough, so I was not sorry when the carts turned up, especially so as we had little or nothing to eat excepting the tiffin we brought along. Some hot tea and a snack was more than acceptable.*

The next day, he left by morning train to Bangkok.

Got home in time for tiffin and very glad. You do appreciate the house after two months jungle travelling and this time I did doubly so as there was much to come back to ..... Both Di and John W. fit and the latter thriving well. Miss Hoyte, one of the nurses from the home had been with them all the time, and her company had done much to make the time pass quickly. Back home too, he had more time to evaluate the journey. *A very pleasant trip all through,* (he seems to have forgotten the constant soaking he received on the return journey) *and, of course, the first part with Prince Damrong was a most well arranged picnic. No hardship or discomfort whatsoever. Everything provided at each stopping place, decent quarters, bathroom, etc. and the table good and plentiful throughout.*

But then he began to consider the cost of the trip.

Transport and everything provided by the Government and everything paid for from central funds. But a lot of it clings to the hands of the petty officials and the labourer, though worthy of his hire, considers himself fortunate if he gets a portion of it. Formerly, he got nothing. The officials kept the lot (and this only a few years ago), but now he does get a bit. As an old Siamese told me, "my people cannot allow any money to pass through their hands without retaining some of it." It's not dishonesty, but the custom of the country – the coolie pays the foreman, the foreman the Inspector, the Inspector the Superintendant and so on up to the Governor. Even to the King. The unsatisfactory part of it all is that amongst the Siamese, commission and bribes are accepted by one and all alike and they look upon any man who does otherwise as a fool for doing so.

Grandfather's comments can be seen in the light of an incident that had happened the previous year when he had the opportunity to line his own pockets. In January of that year, he was working on the Northern Line at Paknam Pho.

To the Treasury at Paknam Pho to draw 40,000 ticals. They handed it over and after signing for it, I took it away to the launch. Whilst waiting in the launch, it struck me as being a lot of notes for the amount. I then checked it and found that I had been paid 72,000 too much, the mistake being in four packets of notes which had been given to me as bundles of 2000, whereas in reality they were bundles of 20,000 ticals. As they were new packets, I had accepted them with only a casual glance. Being (unfortunately for my chances of becoming wealthy) born more or less honest (I hope more), I returned to the Treasury with it. Some days after this, when Müller (Chief Overseer) was talking with the Second Governor about the above matter, he (the latter) remarked, 'What a fool. Why didn't he keep it?'

Notes

1. The 'three little girls' were the princesses Phumphitsamai Diskul ('Poon'), Philailekha Diskul ('Pilai') and Phatthanayu Diskul ('Lua'). They lived and travelled with their father wherever he went and even accompanied him when he was exiled to Pinang in 1932.

   Princess Philailekha Diskul, who was nine at the time of the Southern Peninsula trip, eventually died aged ninety-five in 1992.

2. Grandfather's report and recommendation of Hua Hin is confirmed in the Registry office of Hua Hin (ref. Civil Registry: 2539: 27).

Nong Sala station near Hua Hin circa 1912 and 2012.

CHAPTER EIGHT
PROMOTION & PROTOCOL

In September 1906, grandfather started his new job as Technical Secretary to the Minister of Public Works, Phraya Sukhum.

> *7th. Sept. Started in to work at offices of the Ministry. Don't think there is going to be a lot of work attached to it beyond writing occasional reports and giving opinions on railway subjects.*

He notes down a conversation with Phra Ratha, a Siamese Engineer trained in England, about the expropriation of land for railway requirements and the swindling that went on in the Lands Record Office – not that grandfather was unaware of it. It was common practice for a speculator to buy up land cheaply that looked like it was going to be acquired for railway purposes. A higher price would then be made out for the title deeds and the balance pocketed when the land was needed.

> *Judicious feeing of the government officials is then required so that no questions should be asked why this piece of land should be selling for possibly five or six times the price of adjoining land in the neighbourhood. The same Phra Ratha was telling me about a case he thought of bringing against his brother concerning the ownership of some land left by his father. He remarked that although his case was good and he had sufficient proof to win in any ordinary court, it would most likely be given in favour of his brother, he being rich and able to make friends with the judge, bribe witnesses, etc. He remarked that almost invariably it was useless for a poor man to bring an action against a rich one, as bribery and corruption was just as rife now as in the old days*

As much as he might have disapproved of the way of doing things in Siam, grandfather was not about to try and change it singlehandedly. A conversation with Edward H. Strobel, the veteran American diplomat and legal adviser to the Siamese Government is jotted down.

Mr. Gittins, I never offer advice or make suggestions, tho' I see plenty of points in the Administration that require improvement. When I am asked for my advice or my opinion, I give it to the best of my ability, but I never offer it or make suggestions.

For the rest of the year, he was in Bangkok which he found

somewhat objectionable on account of the enormous cost of everything. House servants etc. are high and it's impossible to save, in fact it means very careful living to keep within one's income.

He was also a little bored.

The work light. Not enough to keep one going in fact. I look upon it as a sort of compensation for the hard work of the past. But what he was still very much involved in was his plan for a Southern Railway Line all the way to the British Federated Malay States. *Wrote a lot about it. Suggested that a separate Department with a Siamese Director should be formed to carry it out and make it entirely independent of the present German controlled one, which if all rumour is true, they must do. For the British are supposed to have laid it down that all railways constructed in the Malay Peninsula must be carried out by engineers of British or Siamese nationality and that no Germans need apply. I made out a proposition for working it and there the matter rests, as it's all connected with the coming new treaty now under consideration.*

Even a meeting with Prince Damrong failed to produce any results.

9th. March 1907. Called on Prince Damrong. Very affable and talkative as usual. Told him of my suggestions for a separate and new Department, with a Siamese head for the Southern Line. He did not agree ..... Time not ripe ..... For the present, it must be under Germans. Could not make a separate Department.

With the negotiations for the new treaty in progress, Prince Damrong was obviously unwilling to commit himself to anything at that stage. In fact, in March 1909, the Anglo-Siamese Treaty was to bring about exactly the plan that grandfather was advocating, only with himself as Controlling Engineer rather than a Siamese head. But all this was still ahead. For the moment, apart from two tours with Prince Nares, (the Minister of Local Government and Police), one to the east and one to the north, where the possibilities of roads and railways were studied, he seems to have been rather marking time and not even a reception for the inauguration of a new palace (Amphon Sathan) at Dusit Park, an area north of the Old City, which the King was developing into new Royal Quarters with boulevards, gardens and palaces, could enthuse him.

This being the night of his (the King's) *first stay, new furniture, new fittings, new beds and without much doubt new wives to fill 'em. Reception included the Foreign Legation people and most of the German officials. A pretty mixed lot and a poor showing anyway. Interior of the palace (very small one, sort of glorified villa) looks well by night. There are some very nice things there in the way of pictures, furniture and curios. All, of course, very clean but it won't remain so for very long. Dirt and betel juice stains will soon alter the present appearance. From the palace downwards, with very few exceptions, the houses of Siamese are more or less filthy. The usual reception rooms do look clean and often well arranged, but look into the dark corners, go behind in the corridors and general rooms, or down below the house and around the premises and filth and dirt is as plentiful as you want it, and a bit more so. Everything is surface. Even at the new palace, the new specially reserved water closets were used (against orders but that means nothing) by the retainers and promptly got choked by bits of stick and other articles used by them.*

Grandfather's strictures concerning the royal palace were almost certainly influenced by the thought that its construction diverted resources from national civil projects, such as building railways. But it was not only the Siamese that came under grandfather's scrutiny.

Too many of the European officials are invited to these shows. Instead of inviting only a few foreign representatives and heads of Departments, they include a lot of juniors, many of whom turn up in the most incongruous dress. Evening dress suit and coloured tie. Frock coats and red leather boots, etc. (mostly Germans who sport this style) with the result that they get treated in rather an offhand sort of way.

It was probably just as well that with little going on in the office and the Southern Railway project still the subject of negotiation between the British and Siamese governments, grandfather took the opportunity of a trip back to England and on the 11th. April 1907 left with his wife and son for a holiday, sailing via Singapore and Colombo on a German mail ship, the 'Zeiten.'

Pleasant enough passage up to Colombo, but we had too many of the beer-swilling, spread napkin, never miss a meal stamp of German on board and they are objectionable. Don't mind a few of them but the ship swarmed with 'em and on leaving Singapore the beer ran down the scuppers from the table when the parting drinks were taken. The smell of it lasted nearly up to Colombo.

On the 21st. April, they arrived at Colombo and put up at the G.O.H. (the Grand Oriental Hotel, close to the port).

A good hotel, but a pig of a German for manager. Why is it that the class of Germans who come East have changed so much in the past twenty years? The early ones were a decent well-mannered lot. The later ones are an overbearing, shouting, push themselves everywhere sort of crew, due I suppose to their coming in such numbers.

Some of grandfather's complaints about the Germans on the trip were due to his dislike of drunkenness and loud behaviour in general. (He had, after all, been very severe with his compatriot Deans in the past.) But they also reflected the increasingly jingoistic tone of the times. Having come late to the colonial race after its unification in 1871 under Bismarck, Germany was keen to catch up, which meant competing aggressively with other powers (especially Britain) for naval and commercial supremacy. Of the latter, grandfather had had plenty of experience with the bitter rivalry for railway concessions in Siam. For the railway market was not only an important outlet for manufacturing industry but a significant factor in determining which of the European powers would have influence in an area.

Fortunately, the rest of the trip seemed to go off without further irritation, except for one typically robust entry in his diary.

Young John rather noisy one night which called forth some loud spoken remarks from some woman in the adjoining cabin, and a few loud remarks in return.

But finally, after a voyage of nearly seven weeks, they reached Southampton on the 28th. May 1907. And it is in England that the diaries finish as does my more intimate knowledge of my grandfather. From then on, I had to rely on newspaper articles, letters and the history of the time for further information.

Laying of rails with chief engineer Henry Gittins looking on.
(Private Collection)

CHAPTER NINE
The southern Line &
World War I

In 1909, the Southern Railway project which my grandfather had proposed to Prince Damrong in 1906, finally fitted in with the finalization of the Anglo-Siamese Treaty, which transferred the four Malay States of Perlis, Kedah, Kelantan and Terengganu which had been under Siamese control to British control in exchange for a loan of four million pounds to build the Southern Railway. Since the early nineteenth century, the British had been keen to develop a trade route from India, through Burma and Siam to Singapore and this now gave them the opportunity to have a vested interest in the link between Bangkok and Singapore, while for the Siamese, the link was just as important for the modernization and development of the Southern peninsula.

A condition of the treaty was that the construction of the railway would have to be under British management and to this end grandfather was appointed head of the new Department as reported in The Bangkok Times of the 27th. August 1909. 'His Majesty the King (Chulalongkorn) has now formally sanctioned the appointment of Mr. Henry Gittins to the post of Controlling Engineer in charge of the Royal Southern Railway Department. In view of his length of service and the importance of the work he has done in the construction of railways in Siam, no more fitting head of the new Department could have been found.'

It was, of course, a major setback for German interests in Siam. Not only was British plant preferred (between 1912-1919 my grandfather ordered forty-two North British E class 4-6-0 locomotives), but work on the Northern Line on which the German contingent was working was shelved for three years, while attention and resources were concentrated on the Southern Line.

The other setback for the German cause was that the Southern Line was built to metre gauge, not the European Standard gauge which the Germans had used on the Northern lines and which had been the subject of much controversy as it differed from neighbouring countries. The German argument for their choice had been that it would make it more difficult for a neighbouring country to overrun Siam, but equally it made it more difficult for Siam to communicate and trade with neighbouring countries. At any rate, some ten years later, all Standard gauge line in Siam began to be converted to metre gauge at enormous cost to the Siamese government. In his book on 'The Railways of Siam', R.Ramaer remarks that 'the German point of view had at last been defeated.'

Having waited so long for a decision over the Southern Line, grandfather was quick to get the project going once the green light had been given. He divided the work into three sections. The first section started from Phetchaburi (as there was already an existing line from Bangkok to Phetchaburi), while the second section started from the south at Singora, leaving the third section to be started from Trang, which at that time was situated on the coast.

Construction work in progress.

Construction pressed ahead rapidly and by March 1911 the line from Trang inland to Tab Thien (which is now the relocated city of Trang) had been completed. A contributor to the Bangkok Times Weekly Mail praised the benefits of the new Trang line as he remembered what the roads were like. 'My men often had to help to extricate bullock carts, sunk axle deep in yellow clay ..... I have had several falls off my pony through this state of affairs, and often had to get off and help to pull him out by the reins.'

By the middle of 1915, the line from Phetchaburi to Singora on the other side of the peninsula had been completed, a distance of 803 kms., while the total track laid (including the Trang branch and other branches and junctions totalled 982 kms. The Bangkok – Khorat line (285kms.) opened in 1900 had taken eight and a half years. Part of the reason for the speed of construction was that running the line close to the coast meant that matcrials could be delivered more easily by boat,

Steel bridge over Pran River. 80m. span.

Below: Steel bridge 4 spans 25m. Petchaburi Division.

but also because the disputes and squabbles between Murray Campbell and Karl Bethge that had bedevilled the Bangkok – Khorat line were absent from the construction of the Southern Line. 'Great credit,' proclaimed the Pinang Gazette, 'is due to the enterprise and organizing skill of Mr. Gittins and his acumen and tactfulness in recruiting an international staff of experienced engineers selected on their individual merits.'

A letter from Prince Damrong, written on the 18th. May 1915, congratulates grandfather ' most heartily on the connection of the lines now completed from Bangkok to Singora, a result of your work and care such as anybody in your position has a full right to be proud of.' He comments also on the improvement of the rolling stock. 'Your new cars are simply perfect. I travelled in one of them from Hua Hin to Bangkok and did not feel the fatigue so much as one tenth as I used to suffer by travelling in the old short car.'

But at the end of 1915, disaster struck. There was unprecedented flooding in the Southern peninsula, particularly in the area south of Patulung. Thirty-six inches of rain fell in four days, causing considerable damage to the new line. The total length affected was about five hundred kilometres, with ten kilometres totally washed away. Nor was the matter helped by an extremely exaggerated account of the damage by a correspondent of the Pinang gazette, who reported that many embankments had been carried away by the flood water, bridges damaged and some carried down river, derailed wagons, drowned cattle and considerable loss of life.

Interviewed about the correspondent's account, grandfather was very firm in repudiating most of the claims. When, for instance, the former had written that 'people from Patulung say the permanent way is washed out over a distance of eighty kilometres and that a large steel bridge at San Keo has been carried one hundred and twenty feet downstream and another smaller steel bridge has gone at Guan Nieng Station,' he replied that 'from Patulung south the permanent way is not washed out for the greater part of eighty kilometres. Less than four kilometres of the banks, and some ballast in other places, have been washed out. The large steel bridge referred to has slipped down at one end, one abutment only having been scoured. When the correspondent ventured to write of forty tons of ironwork being swept one hundred and twenty feet, his imagination was more vigorously active than in most of his many inaccurate statements. No small steel bridge has been carried away at Guan Nieng.'

But the statement that seems to have particularly riled him was the correspondent's assertion that 'to the south of Ootapao on the Pattani main line, I am informed the line is practically wiped out ..... the Siamese engineer on the first section has estimated the damage to his part alone at one million ticals. Mr Gittins said he thought that was a bigger exaggeration than any in the article. In the first forty kilometres, less than one kilometre of bank, in stretches from ten to seventy metres, had been washed out and no bridges of any description were damaged. Mr.Gittins added: I am sure no Siamese engineer made such a preposterous statement as that the damage anywhere amounted to one million. As a matter of fact, to make good the actual damage done by the floods and put the line in the same state as before, from Pattani to Bandon, will not exceed three hundred thousand ticals.

As a parting shot, grandfather added that 'the engineers on the Southern Line, both Siamese and European, are glad to give all information required to responsible persons, but their work is too important to permit of their wasting their time in giving information to any chance-comer.'

The robustness of grandfather's replies disguise the fact that it was obviously a major setback for his project. 'There were floods,' the Pinang Gazette article went on to say, 'generally termed "records" in 1911 and again in 1913, but they were

4th. Class Station.

3rd. Class Station.

2nd. Class Station. (Patalung)

1st. Class Station. (Singora)

child's play compared with the recent devastating outpouring of water.' All the same, to guard against any future freak flooding, he instigated further protection works and increased the flood openings in the embankments and bridges.

By April 1917, the Southern Line had pushed south into Kedah and Kelantan, having divided at Ootapao (the junction for Singora) to run either side of the Malay peninsula. Pinang, on the western side was now connected to Bangkok and half the line had been laid to Kelantan on the other side. Meanwhile, up in the north of Siam, work on the Northern Line had started again in 1912 under the German Director-General Luis Weiler. The construction of the line through the mountainous northern regions had involved much tunnelling, but by 1917 had reached Lampang on the way to Chiang Mai.

It was at this stage that the First World War finally involved Siam, which had until then maintained a careful neutrality. But in April 1917, the United States joined the Allied Powers and the tide of war turned against Germany. King Vajiravudh now saw the advantages of joining the Allied Powers and on the 22nd. July 1917, declared war on Germany.

The previous month, in almost certain preparation for the declaration of war, the Northern and Southern railway lines were amalgamated into one department (the Siamese Royal State Railways) under Prince Purachatra as Commissioner-General with grandfather appointed as Adviser. Prince Purachatra was then thirty-six years old and grandfather fifty-nine. It was the start of a friendly relationship based on mutual respect that was to last to their deaths some twenty years later.

Prince Purachatra (the thirty-fifth son of King Chulalongkorn and step-brother to the King) had been educated in England (Harrow and Trinity College, Cambridge) and was one of the most able members of the government. Although a highly trained soldier, familiar with military engineering, he was new to civil railway work. In one of his first letters (dated 26th. June 1917) that he wrote to my grandfather, he was clearly aware of the extent to which he was going to need his help.

Dear Mr. Gittins,

I had the opportunity of seeing the King yesterday, and had the honour of submitting to His Majesty our plan of amalgamation, which has received the Royal Sanction.

His Majesty is most desirous that you and I should sit together under one roof as soon as possible, in order that I should have you as my right hand man in the reorganization of the Department.

It was soon after his new appointment that grandfather received the strangest commission of his career. A few days before the King's declaration of war on Germany, he was given secret instructions from Prince Purachatra to oversee the internment of all German personnel working on the Northern Line. Dated the 18th. July 1917, the six page 'strictly confidential' letter stipulated that 'the object of your journey will ostensibly be, on taking over the duties of Adviser, that you want to see the construction of the Northern Line.' He was to take with him several Siamese engineers to be ready to replace the German engineers on the 22nd., which was to be the day of internment, and although the Railway Department was not concerned with the arrests, every possible help was to be given if the Military Authorities asked for help.

The 'inspection' was to proceed as far as the line had reached, which was the 1352 metre long Khun Tan tunnel between Lampang and Chiang Mai and which the German Section engineers, Otto Lüders and Emil Eisenhofer had been working on since 1914. As for the actual changeover, 'most of the (Siamese) engineers,' noted Prince Purachatra, 'have high academical qualifications, but have not been given any chance' - a comment that would seem to express a certain departmental frustration at the lack of opportunities offered to Siamese personnel by the German contingent. 'But I feel confident,' continued Prince Purachatra, 'that they will pick up the work very well. They will proceed to their tasks at once.'

Grandfather's role was to see that all the pieces were in place and to oversee the smooth transition from German to Siamese control so that the railway construction could continue as before. It was vital also that the internment could be carried out as swiftly as possible to guard against the possibility of sabotage as it had been known since 1915 that certain German personnel had been hiding weapons and explosives in the jungle on behalf of a band of fugitive Indians who wanted to carry out attacks on the British in India. And although these arms were intended to destabilize the situation in another country, it was always possible that they could have been used to sabotage railway installations.

Besides planning the whole procedure as efficiently as possible, Prince Purachatra also wanted it carried out as correctly as possible, requiring grandfather to arrange a special train to carry the prisoners to Lampang on the same day and 'to arrange, as soon as possible for the families and household effects of the German engineers to be sent to Bangkok, or any other place on the Railway system that they want to, at Railway expense, including porterage.'

For Luis Weiler, the German Director-General, it must have been a sad end to his railway career, but he was a very sick man, and although treated in hospital, did not survive a return voyage to Europe the following year. Another of the German contingent, Emil Eisenhofer, was to receive some years later a compensatory payment from the S.R.R.D. for loss of his job and personal belongings. This so impressed him that he returned to Siam and lived there till his death.

As carefully as the whole operation had been planned, Prince Purachatra finished off the letter by saying that 'these instructions are not to be considered as Orders, binding in every respect, as much depends on circumstances that may arise, beyond what is foreseen. It is for this reason that you, as the senior official next to me in this Department, are selected for this most delicate task. I feel confident that I can rely upon your discretion and your being equal to any emergency, to carry the matter through to the satisfaction of His Majesty's Government.'

Fortunately, there were no emergencies or unforeseen circumstances, and grandfather was able to report back to Prince Purachatra in Bangkok that all had gone according to plan. He would have been less than human though if he had not appreciated the irony of the situation that had at one stroke removed his main competitors in the Railway Department.

With this episode out of the way, attention was returned to completing the Southern Line to the borders of the Federated Malay States. The Kedah connection had actually been unofficially completed in April as reported by the Pinang Gazette on 3rd. April 1917.

'Mr H.Gittins, Chief Engineer of the Siamese State Railways, is spending a few days in Pinang, having come through direct by train from Bangkok, in company with Mr.P.A.Anthony, General Manager of the F.M.S. Railways. The actual journey took less than five days, and was leisurely performed in two inspection carriages, together with a kitchen and servant's car. The trip was rendered possible by the laying of the last rail for connecting the Siamese and F.M.S. systems on Friday last, in the presence, on behalf of Siam, of Mr Gittins and Phya Ramphaipongsi, the Divisional Engineer in charge of the Kedah connection and on behalf of the F.M.S. Government, of Messrs. Anthony, Henshaw and Bilke. It was quite an informal function, and there were no speeches to mark the importance of the occasion.'

After this ceremony, grandfather accompanied Mr.Anthony down through the F.M.S. until they reached Kuala Lumpur via

Taiping, where he met up with his wife who had been visiting Singapore and who now accompanied him back to Bangkok, being the first to travel right through from Singapore to Bangkok by train.

In September of 1917, grandfather accompanied Prince Purachatra in his specially appointed royal saloon car (designed by the London firm of C.P.Sandberg) on a tour of the Southern Siamese and F.M.S. railway systems, following the route he had inspected earlier in the year. It was Prince Purachatra's first official railway tour undertaken under the flag of the new Department and, dressed in full military uniform, he was received with great ceremony at every stop and 'expressed his pleasure at the cordial welcome he received everywhere.' It only remained now to finish off the Southern Line on the Kelantan side of the peninsula to complete the opening up of southern Siam and promote the development of the whole area.

It had been a year full of achievement, and in December, grandfather was awarded The Grand Cross of the Crown of Siam for outstanding services to the Kingdom of Siam. 'My heartiest congratulations,' wrote Prince Purachatra, 'on hearing that His Majesty has decided to honour you by bestowing The Grand Cross of the Order of Siam upon you. The record of your distinguished career, and the important service you are rendering Siam at the present moment, makes His Majesty's choice an eminently suitable and well-deserved one.'

But now, at the height of his career, after thirty years in Siam, his health began to break down more seriously. Another letter from Prince Purachatra, dated 11th. September 1918, is addressed to him in Singapore where he was recuperating. In its concern for his well-being and disclosure of his own health problems, it is evidence of the friendly relationship which had developed between the two men. 'First of all, I want to impress upon you the necessity of you and Mrs.Gittins having a complete rest with the full assurance that during your absence, I will be taking charge in Bangkok all the time ..... I have been missing very much your advice in certain matters, but you may rest assured that things will be kept going.' He goes on to give a summary of the Department's Annual Report, which he was getting ready for publication and then brings up various other matters: the price of mild steel round bars for steel-concrete bridges, a request to grandfather to research a French civil engineering firm working in Singapore for possible competitive quotes and concern about the over-production of rubber in newly established Siamese companies that had sprung up close to the major Southern railway terminals, and so on.

The final part of his letter though, illustrates the tremendous work burden placed on the more able ministers of the Government. After thanking grandfather for his condolences on a family bereavement, he goes on to say, 'what with the worry and the work, it hacked me up for nearly a week, and I had to call in Dr. Smith, who prescribed complete rest and isolation from work. But as I could not take a rest, he prescribed Bromides, which has put me right now, and I feel steadier than I have felt for some time. I know fully well that this course of Bromides does not pay in the long run, so that when you have rested fully and come back again, and after having seen you, I will probably take a rest myself ..... but I do not want you to return without having fully recuperated yourself, because you and I know that the work of the Department is very severe indeed and only a strong constitution can stand the work in your position or in mine.'

The following year, with more health problems, grandfather must have decided to retire, but was persuaded to stay on with a new contract, which increased his salary, finalized his pension and added a gratuity for long service, the period to be 'not less than three years and not more than five years.' This latter stipulation was to cause him some worry, when two years later, his health finally broke down for good and he was forced to retire on medical grounds. But any concern he might have had about not fulfilling the minimum three years was quickly dispelled by Prince Purachatra, who wrote to him on the 25th. March 1921. 'You may rest assured that both (gratuity and pension) will be granted ..... I congratulate you at the appreciation of the Siamese Government for your high and valuable service.'

Grandfather would have undoubtedly continued if he could have done. But he had worked himself to a standstill. A glimpse of the sorry state of his health is given in The Bangkok Times Mail of April 1921. 'Unfortunately, however, for the last six months, his health has been anything but satisfactory and consequently he has been compelled to retire under strong and insistent medical advice. In spite of the fact that latterly he could only with difficulty walk, he was never absent from duty for a single day and attended to his work regularly without a hitch.'

With the news of his resignation, the expressions of regret started to come in from friends, colleagues and superiors. Prince Nares, in a letter dated the 18th.March 1921, wrote that he was 'very sorry indeed for losing you my old, intimate and good friend.' The Engineering Association of Malaya invited him to become an Honorary Member. A letter from The British Club in Bangkok received his letter of resignation with much regret and 'would esteem it an honour if he was to allow his name to remain on the books of the Club.'

After the regrets voiced on his resignation, the tributes to his life and work followed, of which the one that would have meant the most to him, came from the Commissioner-General himself. Summarizing his career, Prince Purachatra commented that 'joining the department from the Railway Surveys in 1892, Mr.

Gittins rose to the highest rank obtainable as Adviser and Chief Engineer to the Department ..... He left Government Service at a time when the Southern Line, over the construction of which he was in charge as Controlling Engineer from the beginning, was practically completed. The fine record of the building of this line will always stand as a monument of his great work in Siam. Not only was his technical opinion much valued on account of his ripe experience of railway practice in Siam, but his sense of fairness, his sound judgement in all matters appertaining to administration, has made his work in the Department most valuable.

He also sat as Technical Adviser to the Commission which drafted the Law on Organization of Railways and Highways, and it has been due to his insight into the working of railways in Siam to the minutest detail that with his advice a law of such technical nature has been so successfully drafted.

Apart from his railway work, all those who came in contact with him have always recognized Mr. Gittins' whole-hearted devotion for Siam and Siamese interests. In Mr. Gittins' retirement, the Government has lost one of its most devoted and capable servants. He takes with him, in his retirement, the best wishes of his colleagues for a long and restful life after his strenuous labours.'

It was time for grandfather to take his leave. A formal presentation by Prince Purachatra of a silver tea and coffee service took place in the offices of the Royal State Railway, and having already taken leave of the King at a garden party, grandfather and his wife boarded the Southern Line train for Pinang for the start of his journey back to England.

At Pinang, he gave a final 'signing-off' interview to the Pinang Gazette in which he remarked that it was now thirty years since the first line was opened from Bangkok and the Siamese in his opinion were now sufficiently experienced to run the railways themselves – and with that endorsement of the system that he had helped to create, it was time to go.

Henry Gittins in court dress.

CHAPTER TEN
*R*ETIREMENT

The early years of retirement were spent in the West Country to be close to where his children were being educated, (a second son, Anthony, had been born in 1910) as other than when they were very young, grandfather had not actually seen them. Medical opinion at that time was that English children should not stay longer in Asian countries beyond the age of six because of the climate and various diseases. So, like many children of expatriates, they had been sent back to England at an early age to boarding school and looked after by relatives during the holidays. And although their mother had returned to England now and again on leave, their father had stayed in Siam, unable and perhaps unwilling to leave due to the demands and responsibilities of his work.

For grandfather, it must have been difficult to come to terms with retirement from the life he had known so long in Siam, although correspondence from friends and colleagues helped to keep him in touch. A letter from Prince Damrong, dated July 7th. 1922, offers grandfather the benefit of his own experience of retirement from public life which had taken place seven years earlier.

'I consider the best reward that a man can get on his retirement is a clear conscience in the recollection of his past works; at all events that is what I enjoy and think that you are in the position to do the same ..... a man who has been accustomed to live an active life must find some sort of things to occupy his mind and keep up the activity. Perhaps gardening, as you said in your letter, that you are occupied with will be beneficial to you, but my dear Gittins, you must not allow yourself to live an idle life which I am certain would make you unhappy.' Prince Damrong himself, had very successfully tackled retirement by taking up a second career as a historian and writer.

Prince Nares, replies to him from Hua Hin. Prince Nares had been the first to build a holiday residence at the little fishing village which grandfather had recommended on his survey for the Southern Line in 1906 and which had become increasingly popular due to its proximity to the capital.

'After having read your letter, I can but feel with appreciation that you still retain your love and affection for Siam.' But like all the most able ministers of the time, the responsibilities of high office had taken their toll on his health too. 'I am approaching my sixty-ninth year and have served as Minister for thirty-seven years. It was very considerate of His Majesty to allow me to take a rest from the labours of State. I may now stay for long periods at Hua Hin, and the rest and sea air, I am certain, can be but beneficial to my health. Like yourself, I may say that we have opened and cleared the ground for the future prosperity of Siam and done our work to the best of our ability. It is for the younger generation now to sow and reap on the ground.'

But it was his correspondence with Prince Purachatra that would have meant the most to him. Early in 1922, Lord Northcliffe (the Press baron, Alfred Harmsworth) had written an article for the Daily Mail, describing his train journey through the Far East and singling out in particular the Siamese State Railways for their 'wonderful smoothness of running ..... one of the most peaceful and comfortable train journeys I can remember,' helped, no doubt, by the loan of Prince Purachatra's private saloon car. He also wrote appreciatively of the system of rest-houses for overnight accommodation which punctuated the line.

'At the time of my journey, trains did not run at night on account of the possibility of colliding with elephants and buffaloes straying across the line, and they used to stop every evening at about six or seven o'clock at a country station where there was a rest-house for passengers to sleep in. A through service was to be inaugurated on January 2nd. of this year.' (A service which grandfather had been keen to promote before his retirement by the introduction of sleeping and restaurant cars.)

'The rest-houses,' continued Lord Northcliffe, 'are a series of little bungalows, each containing two double rooms, two bathrooms, and a small compound. A covered way usually connects bungalow with bungalow. There is also a kind of parent bungalow, where you can get meals, and whence coffee and shaving water are issued to the sleeping bungalows in the morning. It is really charming to alight from the hot train before one of these tiny garden cities, spend an hour or two wandering about in the cool of the evening and, after dinner, to drop luxuriously into a real bed and fall asleep to the tiny voices of the jungle, with fireflies round your mosquito net as nightlights.'

In writing to grandfather to tell him about Lord Northcliffe's account, Prince Purachatra generously gives him all the credit. 'I have been most gratified by Lord Northcliffe's attention in regard to the Siam State Railways and we all feel that the honour of the Southern Line belongs to you, for I took over when it was practically completed and all the spade work had been done.'

In a later letter that year, Prince Purachatra gives further evidence of the friendly and respectful relationship between the two men when he says, 'I am always glad to receive any observations or criticisms – even adverse ones – from you as during our relationship in the Department you have always talked freely to me and it is arising out of these observations that outlook on things can be broadened and the pros and cons of the question fully studied.'

In the same letter, Prince Purachatra voices his concern

over the grave financial situation in Siam. A succession of bad rice crops (which accounted for 80% of Siam's export revenue) and the general slump in world trade had forced Siam to borrow from the financial markets. But he is at pains to reassure grandfather that railway plans were still on course. 'The ten year programme for railway construction has already been fixed and approved by His Majesty's Government and so far as I am aware, there has been no change in the policy or curtailment due to necessity of withdrawal of loan funds new or old for other purposes.'

Finishing off his letter, Prince Purachatra adds a little personal comment as to his method of dealing with the stress of his job. 'You will be interested to hear that I have taken up golf in addition to my tennis. These things take my mind off my work out of office hours and that is the secret I am able to do any work at all.'

An early visitor was a Siamese engineer, Luang Prakit, who had accompanied him at the time of the internment of the German engineers in 1917 and who stayed with grandfather in Devon for a few days in January 1922. He had been sent to England by Prince Purachatra to study railway matters at the Consulting and Inspecting Engineers firm of C.P.Sandberg, whom grandfather had introduced into Siam. As a result of this visit, the possibility of a consultant's role seems to have been aired. In a letter to grandfather, dated 21st. January 1922, C.P.Sandberg, son of the original founder, wrote:

'We were delighted to hear that he (Luang Prakit) had been staying with you and that he found you well. He mentioned that he quite recognized that all your valuable experience of Siam should not be lost and that he was going to suggest to Prince Purachatra that you should act in some capacity. It seems to me that this should be a very great advantage to Siam. It would certainly be of help to me and it would perhaps give you a certain amount of interesting work .... We, personally, would be very glad to ask for your professional advice and have the benefit of your local knowledge on a business understanding between us .... We have so much to thank you for, such as the valuable introduction to Siam and many years of pleasant work.'

Although no formal arrangement seems to have come of Sandberg's suggestion, he wrote again in April to say that he had received a letter from Prince Purachatra in which he hoped that Sandbergs kept in touch with grandfather as 'he is a mine of valuable information as regards to the local conditions obtaining in Siam and besides, he is one of those Europeans whom not only myself who have come in close contact, but the Siamese generally have the very deepest respect for his honesty and integrity and the solid work he has done for Siam.'

Over the next few years, grandfather kept up a regular correspondence with Prince Purachatra, meeting the Prince in London when he paid visits to Europe. In 1929, the latter wrote to grandfather with the news of his award of two commemorative medals sent 'under His Majesty's command for valuable assistance in bringing about the successful completion of the Bangkok Memorial Bridge.' The medals were to be the last honours that he received from the Siamese Government.

The following year, his wife persuaded him to move to London, where they took up residence in Bramham Gardens and although it must have been easier to welcome and keep in touch with friends, he was not a city person at heart. It must have been with some relief that in May 1931 he accompanied his wife and their future daughter-in-law, Anne, on a voyage to Fiji for her marriage to their eldest son, John, who was a junior cadet in the Colonial Administrative Service.

In her book, 'Tales of the Fiji Islands', my mother records that her parents-in-law stayed on in Fiji for several weeks after the wedding in the capital Suva and that they then visited the newly-wed couple on their first official posting on Kadavu island, some fifty miles south of the capital. When it was eventually time for the parents-in-law to return to Suva, 'they bravely agreed to sail in a small banana cutter. This needed some courage for a couple of their age, for some of the cutters were old, not too clean, smelled of oil and copra and were overrun with cockroaches. Above the water line there was only a small cabin belonging to the captain, no 'mod-cons' of any sort, and no privacy for women passengers.

I packed up some food for them as the boat was to collect bananas all day from villages up the coast before crossing to Suva. I did not think that the curry made by the crew for the captain and themselves would be very appetising, mingling with the smell of diesel oil, wet rope, copra, stale fish, dirty clothes, kerosene and the stale perspiration of the crew.

At 4.0 a.m. we trekked down to the beach by the light of hurricane lanterns and found the boat waiting. I gave my mother-in-law an empty 7lb. biscuit tin.

"You will need this," I said, "as the journey takes about nineteen hours before you arrive in Suva!" '

I am not sure about my grandmother, but I am sure my grandfather would have been quite happy with the arrangement. After all, it would have seemed just like old times.

Back in London, grandfather kept up his lifetime's habit of walking most days, even if for someone who, as the Bangkok Times said, ' had walked practically all over Siam', he was now limited to exploring the London parks. A portrait of him at this time is given by a relative who recalls that he 'never passed by or brushed off a beggar, saying who was he to judge whether their need was genuine or faked. He had a special pocket in his waistcoat in which he kept all his small change so that he could always reach and produce something.'

In 1932, an event occurred which would have caused him considerable anxiety. A *coup d'etat* in Siam brought about the end of absolute monarchy and introduced a new, constitutional state with power in the hands of a People's Party (Khana Ratsadon), composed of civilians and disaffected military officers. Many of the princes with whom grandfather had been friendly, went into exile, some voluntarily, some under compulsion. Prince Damrong was exiled to Pinang, while Prince Purachatra went with his family to live in Singapore. Although grandfather's immediate worry as to whether his pension would continue to be paid proved unfounded, the upheaval and changes in the country which he had known for more than thirty years would have affected him deeply.

It was perhaps to deflect his thoughts from the present and from encroaching old age that grandfather started his Canadian memoirs, which would have taken him back in his mind to when he was a young adventurer, fit and strong, setting off on his travels. I can see him, neatly dressed in suit and tie, sitting down at his desk with the little brass letter-scales and silver-topped inkwell that are now in front of me. He still had his old notebooks from that time and with these to refer to he took up his pen and with no great preamble started straight in.

11th. March 1934

Wonder if my memory will carry me back to the days I spent in Canada between 1881 & 1885. Let's try. 'Twas in July 1881, that I left England......'

Henry Gittins and sons.

Postscript

My grandfather died in February 1937, aged seventy-eight. In a strange quirk of fate that was noted by many, Prince Purachatra, who had died at the end of the previous year aged fifty-four, was cremated on the same day as grandfather died. 'A coincidence,' as The Bangkok Times noted, 'which will strike all who remember the two men and their close association over so many years in Siam.'

For Prince Purachatra's son, Prem, ' the news came as a sudden shock, and we were all very upset. We looked on Mr. Gittins as one of our dearest friends, and especially in my case. He was very kind to me, helped me in so many ways and taught me so much, that his passing is a severe blow to me. Coming as it does close on my father's death, I feel that a double sorrow has been inflicted on me.'

Finally, in as fine a tribute as anyone would wish to be remembered by, Peter Sandberg, writing on behalf of his brother Alec and himself, summed up what everyone seemed to feel:

'To us, as we have so often remarked to each other, he was so near perfection of what a man should be and could be, that we have never known anyone, except our own father, to equal his qualities.

It will indeed be difficult for those who eventually write an obituary notice to do him justice, but those who knew him will always remember what a great gentleman he was, his honesty, his kind heart, his fearlessness, combined with human understanding and diplomacy. Surely few men have had so many great qualities ....'

Henry Gittins (1858-1937).

Obituary

MR. HENRY GITTINS

"Times" ——— 13. Feb.

BUILDER OF SIAMESE RAILWAYS 1937.

Mr. Henry Gittins, late Adviser to the Siamese State Railways, who died recently at his home in London at the age of 78, had a remarkable career as organizer and builder of railways in Siam.

Born at Clifton, he was articled to a firm of architects at Bristol, but at the age of 24 went to Canada and there specialized in railway work. In 1876 the Governor of the Straits Settlements, during a visit to Bangkok, received from the King of Siam a concession to make surveys for a railway in that country. Twelve years later a British firm, to whom the concession had been assigned, began operations, and among the engineers they engaged was Gittins, not long returned from Canada to England with already some reputation in the railway world. As a junior assistant he drove the first peg in what became a great enterprise, and led him, through many trials and anxieties, to the front rank of his profession.

The survey having been completed, a contract to build the line was given to an Englishman, while, for political reasons which Siam would have avoided but could not, a German engineer was appointed to organize a Government Railway Department to supervise the contractor. This resulted, after a period of bitterness, and recrimination, in the cancellation of the contract, and the State Department took over the construction work. The services of Gittins, who had earned much credit while on the original survey, were eagerly sought by both the contractor and the Department: he joined the latter in May, 1892. In the years that followed he worked in many parts of the country and in all branches of the Department, passing rapidly from grade to grade until, in 1905, he was the senior divisional engineer and the next for appointment as deputy director, with the directorship to follow as a matter of course. But it was desired in the highest German quarters to make the Royal Siamese State Railways as far as possible a German enclave, and the director now informed the Government that if a British deputy director were appointed, he and most of his men would resign. To save the Department from disruption and the State from a diplomatic imbroglio, Gittins was withdrawn from the executive, but appointed adviser to the Minister in control of communications, including the railways. It says much for his tact and discretion that in this new capacity, which gave him vicarious authority over the whole Department, he continued in amicable relations with the director and his erstwhile colleagues.

In 1909 Siam undertook, with British financial assistance, to complete a railway southwards from Bangkok to the frontier of British Malaya, and for this purpose a separate Department, free from German influence, was established. Gittins, who had personally explored the whole of this proposed route and who was by now recognized as the first authority on Siamese railway construction, became the head of the new Department, and within seven years built and opened for traffic 800 miles of line unsurpassed in construction, equipment, and organization by any railway in the East.

In 1917 Siam joined the Allies in the War, when the Germans in Government employ all disappeared, and by a Royal decree the two railway systems were amalgamated, with Prince Purachatra as Commissioner-General and Gittins as his consulting engineer and adviser. The Prince, who had been to Harrow and Cambridge, and had served with the Royal Engineers, and the adviser, with his long experience and study, worked together with mutual confidence and an immense enthusiasm. They soon welded the various lines into a homogeneous system, and brought the Department, officered by Englishmen and an increasing number of foreign-trained Siamese engineers, to a high state of efficiency.

In 1922, at the age of 64, after 30 years of arduous life in the tropics, Gittins retired, to the great regret of his hosts of friends in Siam, more especially of the Prince and his beloved Department, and came home to England where two years of country life restored his health almost completely. Afterwards he travelled a good deal, and ultimately settled in London. Siamese affairs continued to interest him, and his advice on engineering matters was frequently sought by the Government. Among his decorations were the grand crosses of the White Elephant and the Crown of Siam, and he was made a C.B.E. in 1920. Prince Purachatra remained his close friend until he died last September.

Gittins married and had two sons. Slight, erect, alert of eye and movement, with moustache cocked and little imperial jutting, there was a touch about him of the Elizabethan hero. He read much and had leanings towards poetry and romance, which he concealed from the public behind a certain brusqueness of manner and deportment. An entirely lovable man, with an easy dignity, he upheld in a foreign land the honour and prestige of his country.

Henry Gittins' Decorations

1898   Order of the White Elephant   4th.Class
1906   Order of the Crown of Siam   3rd.Class
1915   Order of the Crown of Siam   2nd.Class
1917   Order of the White Elephant   2nd.Class
1918   Order of the Crown of Siam   1st. Class
1920   C.B.E.

Siamese Monarchy

King Rama iv (Mongkut)   1851-1868
King Rama v (Chulalongkorn)   1868-1910
King Rama vi (Vajiradvudh)   1910-1925
King Rama vii(Prajadhipok)   1925-1934

The country's official name was Siam until 1939, when it was changed to Thailand. It briefly reverted to Siam between 1945-49, but was then renamed Thailand.

Prince Purachatra Jayakara 1881-1936

Prince Purachatra, the thirty-fifth son of King Chulalongkorn was educated in England at Harrow and Trinity College, Cambridge where he studied engineering. He continued this interest when he returned to Siam in 1904 as a military engineer in the Siamese Royal Army.

In 1917, his step-brother, King Vajiradvudh, appointed him Commissioner- General of the Royal State Railways Department, which up until then had been divided into two sections (Northern and Southern) under the control of the Ministry of Public Works. He was responsible for the development of the railway system north to Chiang Mai, north-east to Ubon Ratchathani and east to the Cambodian border at Aranyaprathet.

'To my friend and Adviser, Henry Gittins. In souvenir of our joint work and responsibilities.' Purachatra 8/4/1923.

In 1921, he started the construction of the Railway Hotel at Hua Hin, which was opened in 1923 to give accommodation to passengers taking a break at Hua Hin on the increasingly popular Southern Line.

In the coup d'etat of 1932, it was perhaps appropriate that Prince Purachatra was able to escape from Bangkok on one of his trains to warn the King who was holidaying at Hua Hin, even though his action did not prevent the eventual outcome. The following year, with the new constitution in place, he moved to Singapore with his family, where he died three years later, aged fifty-four.

Prince Purachatra was also notable for his introduction of the first radio broadcasting service in Siam and for his interest, together with his brother, Prince Chakrabongse, in developing aviation. There is a photograph taken in 1911 of him sitting in an early biplane – but in full military uniform.

Prince Damrong Rajanubhab 1862-1943

Prince Damrong, a son of King Mongkut, was known as the second most powerful person in Siam after his half-brother, King Chulalongkorn. As the Minister of Interior (an appointment made when he was only twenty-eight), he was instrumental in transforming Siam from a feudal to a modern state by his reorganization of the provincial administration (see beginning of Chapter Six). Although it was not a policy that could be imposed all at once over the country as there were not enough trained officials to implement the new system, (not to mention opposition from the old provincial nobility), the reforms laid the foundation for a modern central administration.

Prince Damrong and daughters. London 1930.

Amongst his many other appointments were Army Chief, President of the Royal Institute and member of the Supreme Council of State.

In 1915, Prince Damrong resigned from his post at the Ministry and began a highly successful second career as a writer, becoming an authority on Siamese history, culture and religion. His old home, Varadis Palace, is now a museum dedicated to his works.

After the coup d'etat of 1932, which ended the absolute monarchy in Siam, he was exiled to Pinang, although in 1942 he was allowed to return to Bangkok, where he died one year later at the age of eighty-one.

In 1962, UNESCO included him on its list of 'World's Most Important Persons' , the first Thai to achieve this distinction. The day of his death, December 1st., is now officially known as 'Damrong Rajanubhab Day.'

GLOSSARY OF COLLOQUIAL AND SLANG TERMS OF THE TIME

blackguard	=	scoundrel, criminal
cotton	=	take a liking to
damper	=	an unleavened cake made of flour and water & baked in hot ashes
dicky	=	shaky
dunnage	=	baggage
fatherland	=	a person's native country, (especially Germany)
finicking	=	overparticular, fastidious
footling	=	trivial, silly
fossick	=	search, rummage about
hacked me up	=	a short, dry cough, 'affected me'
ilk	=	the same person or thing
in the soup	=	in trouble
isinglass	=	a gelatinous substance used in cookery
scoot	=	run away hurriedly
smudge fire	=	a smoky fire lit as a means of keeping off insects
tiffin	=	lunch
turned me up	=	made me vomit
vamoosed	=	made off (from the Spanish 'vamos')

BIBLIOGRAPHY

Surveying and Exploring in Siam by James McCarthy. Reprint White Lotus. Bangkok. 1994.

Five Years in Siam by H. Warington Smyth. Reprint White Lotus. Bangkok 1994.

Bangkok in 1892 by Lucien Fournereau. White Lotus. Bangkok. 1998.

The Provincial Administration of Siam 1892-1915 by Tej Bunnag. O.U.P. 1977.

The Railways of Thailand by R. Ramaer. White Lotus. Bangkok. 1994.

Tales of the Fiji Islands by Anne Gittins. Acorn Books. 1991.

INDEX

Adelphi Hotel, Liverpool 29
Advisers, foreign 89
Altman 17, 87
Anglo-Siamese Treaty (1909) 111, 115
Anthony P.A. 125
Ayutthaya 13, 51, 59, 61

Baker,Herbert 45
Bandon (Surat Thani) 100-1, 119
Bang Pakong River 86, 88
Bang Saphan 102
Bangkok 19, 22-3, 51, 59, 61-2, 65, 71, 82, 86, 93, 105, 110
Bangkok Times 75-6, 136, 139
Bangkok Memorial bridge 135
Bangkok Times Mail 128
Battleford 32, 35, 37-41
Bethge, Karl 16, 23, 51, 55, 66-7, 75-6, 118
Birtle 32
Bismarck 113
Boyle 38-9
Braddock,Dr. 93, 95
Bramham Gardens 135
Brandon 32
British Club, Bangkok 128
British East India Co. 13
Buddha, footprint 71; tablets, 97
Burma 15, 101, 115

Caldwell, Miss E. 65, 71
Campbell,George Murray 15-7, 19, 66, 74-6, 118
Canadian Pacific Railway Co. 13, 32, 46, 48
Cantlie,Dr. 25-6, 64
Carlton 42-3
Cha-Am 105
Chaiya 101

Chakrabongse, Prince 143
Chao Phraya River (Menam) 18, 20, 23
Chawang 101
Chitr 51
Chonnabot 58
Chulalongkorn, King 13, 15, 67, 85, 89, 93, 111, 115, 122, 142, 144
Chumpawn (Chumphon) 94, 102
Clarkes Crossing 32
Clifton 29, 48, 55
Coolies 10, 54, 63, 84, 88, 96
Colombo 112-3
Corruption 79-80, 106, 109

Dalamain 31, 36, 38
Damrong,Prince 85-6, 93, 95, 99, 100, 106, 110-11, 115, 118, 131, 137 (Appendix 144-5)
Darling & Curry 30, 45
Deans 51-2, 54, 113
Dominion Lands Act of 1872 31
Dong Phya Fai 75
Dusit Park 111

Eagle Hills 38, 41, 43-4
Eisenhofer 123-4
Elephant transport 95, 100, 102-3
Ellis 41, 45

F.M.S. (Federated Malay States) 110, 125
Fiji 135
First World War 122
Fort Ellis 32, 35-6
Fournereau, Lucien 62, 86

Galway, William 14, 63

Gehrts 66, 75-6, 80-1, 85
Gittins,Anne 135-6
Gittins, Anthony 131
Gittins, Daniel, (father) 29
Gittins, Henry (1858-1937),
joins Punchard survey
13-4; with George Murray
Campbell 16; joins Royal
Railways Department 17;
quarrels with Rohns 17,
20; Section Engineer Hinlap
18; visits Ko Sichang 20;
witnesses Paknam Incident,
23-5; convalescence in
Hongkong 25; sails from
Liverpool 29; joins Darling
& Curry 30; joins Soule &
Dalamain 31; ox trek 31-7;
farm work with Boyle 38-9;
encounters with Indians
39; lodges with Parker 39;
evening entertainment in
Battleford 40-1; surveying
work with Ellis 41-5;
attends Jim Suave's
marriage 42; meets Chief
Mosquito 43-4; starts work
on the Ontario & Quebec
railway 45; first job with
C.P.R. 46-8; returns to
England(1885) 48; leaves
for Siam 48; trouble with
colleagues 52-3; survey
to Nong Khai (Laos) 55;
attends Laotian wedding 58;
attends Royal Opening
of Bangkok-Ayutthaya
line (1897) 66-7; home
leave 67-9; i/c Pak Preo
(Saraburi) section 71;
visits Phra Phuttabat 71-2;
witnesses armed robbery
72; marriage 74; comments
on Campbell's court case
75; tribute to Bethge 76;
court case Paknam Pho

(Nakhon Sawan) 79; death
of first child 82; visits jail
at Paknam Pho 84-5; Royal
line opening to Paknam Pho
Oct. 1905 85; promotion to
Division Engineer 85; trip
on ferry launch 'Paet Riu'
87-8; offered new post as
Technical Secretary to the
P.W.D. 88-9; birth of first
son, John Wansbrough 90;
Peninsular trip 93-107;
starts new job as Technical
Secretary 109; Royal
Reception Dusit Park 111-2;
home leave1907 112-3;
appointment as Controlling
Engineer Royal Southern
Railway Dept. 115; begins
construction of Southern
Line 116; flood disaster
118-9; appointed Adviser
to Prince Purachatra 122;
secret orders 123-4; opening
of Bangkok – Pinang Line
125; awarded Grand Cross
of the Order of Siam 126;
breakdown of health 126-8;
resigns 128; leaves Siam
129; retirement 131-7;
visit to Fiji 135-6; starts
Canadian memoirs 137;
death 139
Gittins, John Wansbrough 90,
106, 113, 135
G.O.H. (Grand Oriental Hotel),
Colombo 113
Gowan,Dr. 20-1
Gwennie, death of 82

Hayes, Dr. 22, 51, 82
Hinlap 18, 21, 23, 52
Hong Kong 23-5, 51, 64, 74, 76
Hoyte, nurse 106
Hua Hin 104-5, 118, 132, 143
Humboldt 19

Hynes 42

Indians 39, 42-5

Jubilee, Queen Victoria's 69

Kaeng Khoi 18-9, 51
Kaeppler 22-3, 52-4
Kaiser Wilhelm II 76-7
Kedah 115, 122, 125
Kelantan 115, 122, 126
Khana Ratsada 137
Khao Khao (Huai Yot) 96, 98
Khao Lung National Park 95
Khao Thong pass 100
Khorat (Nakhon Ratchasima)
    13, 51, 56, 58-9, 73
Khun Tan tunnel 123
Kipling, Rudyard 64
Kloke 80
Knight, Mr. & Mrs. 19
Koh Pinnan (Ko Phangan) 94
Kolak (Prachuap Khirikhan)
    102-3
Ko Sichang 20, 24, 64
Kuala Lumpur 125
Kuiburi 104

Lambert, surveying colleague
    19, 22
Lampang 122-4
Lang Suan 102
Laos 24, 55-6, 58
Line opening, (1897) 66-7;
    (1905) 85
Liverpool 29
London 69, 135
Longfellow 82
Lopburi 73, 76
Lucy, sister 81-2
Lüders, Otto 123
Lumsden 45

MacGlashan 18, 51, 61
McCarthy, James 15, 20

Markham, Ontario 45-6
Mekong River 55-6
Mongkut, King 13, 89, 144
Montreal 30
Mosquito, Chief 43, 45
Muak Lek 52-3, 62

Nakhon (Nakhon Si
    Thammarat) 95-6, 100
Nares, Prince, (Minister of Public
    Works) 81, 111, 128, 132
Nong Khai 55-9, 61
Northcliffe, Viscount (Alfred
    Harmsworth) 132-3
Northern Line 80, 107, 122
NorthWest Rebellion 44

Ontario & Quebec Railway 45
Ootapao (Hat Yai) 119, 122

Paet Riu (Chachoengsao) 86
Paknam 88, 93
Paknam Incident 23-5
Paknam Pho (Nakhon Sawan)
    73, 79-80, 82-6, 107
Pak Preo (Saraburi) 16, 18,
    59, 71
Parker 39-40
Patulung (Pattalung) 99, 100,
    118-9
Pattani 100, 119
Payne, i/c Indian Reservation
    43-4
Peak,The (Hong Kong) 25, 65
Perlis 115
Perry Davis Pain Killer 40, 42
Phachi 73
Phaulkon (Chief Minister) 73
Phetchaburi 99, 100, 103-5,
    116
Phichit 57
Phitsanulok 80-1
Phra Phuttabat 71
Phuket 96, 98-9
Pinang 122, 129

Pinang Gazette 118-9, 125, 129
Polynesian,S.S. 29
Portage la Prairie 31-2, 35
Plymouth 68
Prachak, Prince 55-6
Prairie West 29
Prakit, Luang 134
Pranburi 104
Prasidt, Phya, Commissioner at Khorat 58
Prem, Prince 139
Preuss, photographer 93, 95
Punchard (Punchard, MacTaggart & Lowther) 13-16, 75
Purachatra, Prince 105, 122-9, 132-5, 137, 139 (Appendix 142-3)

Quebec 29-30

Raffles 74
Railway Hotel 105, 143
Ramaer, R. 116
Ramphaipongsi, Phya 125
Rapid City 32
Ratha, Phra 109
Ratsada, Phya 96
Revolution 1932 137
Rodrigues 72
Rohns 16-7, 20, 22-3, 87
Ron Phibun 96
Royal Railways Dept. 16, 51, 89-90
Royal Southern Railway Dept. 115

Sam Roi Yot 104
Sandberg,C.P. 126, 134-5, 139
Saskatchewan River 37
Sawi 102
Singapore 65, 112, 126
Singora (Songkhla) 99, 100, 116-8

Si Racha 83, 86
Smiles 63-4, 80
Smith, Dr. 127
Smyth, H.Warrington 56, 75
Soule & Dalamain 31
Soulter 32, 35
Stoney Tribe 43
Strobel, Edward H., American diplomat 110
Suave, Jim 42
Sudbury 32
Sukham,Phya 109
Swallows' nests 94
Swatow (Shantou) 65

Tab Thien (Trang) 98, 117
Tarua (Tha Rua) 18, 73
Terengganu 115
Tha Yang 105
Times, The 11, 89-90
Tin mines 96, 98-9
Toronto 30, 45
Touchwood, Indian reservation 36
Trang 98-9, 116-7

Udon Thani 55
United States 122

Vajiravudh, King 105, 122, 142
Vajirunhis, Crown Prince 61
Varadis Palace 145
Victoria, Queen 13

Wansbrough, Gertrude, ('Di') 55, 71, 74, 76, 82-3, 86, 106, 126-7, 135-6
Weiler 52, 76, 80, 85, 122, 124
Winnipeg 31